BALUCHI WOVEN TREASURES

by Jeff W. Boucher

Published by Jeff W. Boucher
Alexandria, Virginia, USA.

B A L U C H I   W O V E N   T R E A S U R E S

© 1989 by the publisher, Jeff W. Boucher,
250 S. Reynolds, Alexandria, Virginia 22304, USA.

Library of Congress Catalogue Card Number 89-092134

ISBN 0-9623893-0-7

Photography by Garry Muse, London.
Additional photography by Peter John Gates, London (Plates 23, 24, 35, 56 & 61);
Raymond Schwartz, Washington D.C. (Plates 4, 7, 25, 36, 37 & 50).

Packaged by Hali Publications Limited, London, publishers of
HALI, *The International Magazine of Fine Carpets and Textiles*

Designed by Liz Dixon.

Phototypeset in Great Britain.

Printed in Singapore.

*Rugs in this collection are to be exhibited in November 1990 by The Marin Cultural Center & Museum,
Ross, California, at the time of the 6th International Conference on Oriental Carpets (I.C.O.C.) in San
Francisco, California.*

CONTENTS

FOREWORD
Colonel Jeff Boucher, A Collector's Collector

THE LATE GEORGE APLEY, John P. Marquand's incarnation of self-conscious brahminism, studied and acquired Chinese bronzes – not out of predilection, but because he felt that his large collection would fill an obvious gap in the holdings of the Boston Museum of Fine Arts, while at the same time providing needed occupation for scholars.

As Marquand's irony implies, this gelid approach to connoisseurship reduces it – like most of Apley's other activities and benefactions – to the status of grim civic duty. Real collecting, however, is a joyful pursuit, and the desire to collect objects of value – be they baseball cards, butterflies, or fine old Baluchi rugs – is instinctual. The true collector is thus an enthusiast and a sportsman in the highest degree. "After love," said A.S.W. Rosenbach, the great book collector, "collecting is the most exhilarating sport of all."

Colonel Jeff Boucher has been engaged in this sport nearly all of his life. As a young boy on a farm in Texas, he collected Indian arrowheads that turned up in eroded fields. Later, when Indian head pennies began to grow scarce, he collected them too. As a youth with a grey mustang pony of his very own, he quite naturally felt great nostalgia for the Old West and for the great American hero, the cowboy – both disappearing – even then – into song and story; consequently, he eventually collected over five hundred cowboy songs and Western ballads. As a young man, when serving as Secretary of the Mississippi River Commision for the US Army Corps of Engineers, he developed an interest in another vanished world, the ante-bellum American South, and began to collect books on life and literature of the period.

All of these collections followed a similar pattern: each was prompted by the desire to preserve something of value which has passed – or is passing – into oblivion.

While serving as Commander of a Combat Engineer Battalion in Germany in 1951, Colonel Boucher caught sight of more elusive 'prey': he bought three Baluchi rugs. Naturally, no-one with his collecting instincts could long be content with only three charming examples of the weavers' art, and the focus of his collecting efforts soon changed to oriental rugs. Between 1960 and 1967 his worldwide assignments for the US Army and the World Bank enabled him to track his prey through Eastern bazaars. Meeting the late H. McCoy Jones, whose splendid (and extensive) collection of tribal rugs is now the pride of the M.H. De Young Memorial Museum in San Francisco, caused him to narrow the focus of his collection in 1963 and to concentrate on fine, early tribal and nomadic pieces. Between 1971 and 1976 Boucher and McCoy Jones co-authored six catalogues for the annual exhibitions of tribal rugs sponsored by the International Hajji Baba Society in Washington D.C. Since 1974, when they mounted a show of Baluchi rugs, Boucher has devoted himself exclusively to fine old examples.

The elusive Baluchi people who weave most of the pile rugs so admired by collectors are a group of semi-nomadic, non-Turkoman tribes and sub-tribes who live in the area on the borders between Afghanistan and Iran. Though the smouldering beauty of an old Baluchi carpet is quite irresistible when direct sunlight sets its brilliant blue-dyed wool ablaze, this rug type had little commercial value (and attracted little scholarly attention) before the 1960s. Most old Baluchi pieces, easily identifiable by their sombre palette and soft lustrous wool, were made for the weaver's own use. Because high quality Baluchi weavings were never exported in great numbers, it is now more difficult to find them in Europe and America than it is to locate good Caucasian and Turkoman pieces. Therefore serious collectors of Baluchi rugs must often travel great distances in order to assemble a great collection – the kind of collection, that is, which not only awes us by the beauty of the individual pieces it contains, but also adds significantly to our knowledge of the culture that produced them.

George Apley made a large collection of Chinese bronzes. Jeff Boucher, on the other hand, belongs in the company of collectors like H. McCoy Jones, and has made a great collection of Baluchi rugs, one that preserves the finest achievements of a weaving tradition which will soon be only a memory.

Barry Jacobs
Montclair, New Jersey, September 1988

PREFACE

THINGS HAVE MOVED ON apace since 1976, when David Black and Clive Loveless published their memorable *Rugs of the Wandering Baluchi* and everything that *looked* as if it might be Baluch was, indeed, just that. Vague mutterings about Timuris and Arabs and Aimaqs could be heard, but no-one, to be frank, took much notice.

It now seems that any weaving made in east Iran or west Afghanistan, which could not be attributed with confidence to any other tribal group, was hastily catalogued as 'Baluch' and left to find its place in the market. Since that market was largely populated by individuals such as Jeff Boucher and myself, who were generally considered by the older dealers to be scraping the bottom of the barrel and certifiable to boot, I don't suppose anyone thought it mattered too much.

Even so, anyone who has collected 'Baluch' rugs – and the last decade has seen a growing number of recruits to the ranks – must have become aware, sooner or later, that everything he or she had acquired did not quite fit together. I remember quite early on in my career as a Baluchiphile poring over an illustration on page 125 of *The Colour Treasury of Oriental Rugs* by Stefan A. Milhofer (Oxford 1976), which the author, in understandable puzzlement, had described as "Kirghiz. East Turkestan". Its field consists of three vertically arranged panels of a design obviously related to the composition found on one of the best-known groups of Baluch *khorjin*, of which three examples, plates 33-35, are in the Boucher collection.

The Milhofer rug, however, is quite clearly something very different. An examination of the only comparable example I have seen, which appeared in a London auction a couple of years ago (Phillips, 30th September 1986, lot 84), suggests that it is Kurdish, or 'Kordi', to use the Farsi word popularised by Wilfried Stanzer in his excellent and innovative monograph *Kordi: Lives, Rugs, Flatweaves of the Kurds in Khorasan* (Vienna 1988). However, I am still not entirely confident of this attribution, especially as Colonel Boucher has described a fourth, and complete, *khorjin* of this design in his collection, plate 58, as Timuri work by the Dokhtar-e-Ghazi from the Gulran area of Herat Province in northwest Afghanistan (you can't get much more specific than that!).

I am, in other words, admitting to a certain amount of personal confusion. Despite the sterling work done in recent years by Messrs. Janata, Wegner, Craycraft, Stanzer and many others on the weavings of the east Iranian/west Afghani tribes, attributions still remain elusive and somewhat subjective. Indeed, Michael Craycraft, in a recent catalogue published by the Adraskand Gallery in California, *Belouch and Karai Rugs of Torbat-i-Heydarieh*, suggests that much of what we had fondly thought to be indubitably 'Baluch' is no such thing (I use the slightly prevaricatory inverted commas to save arguments).

According to Mr Craycraft, the Karai were the dominant tribe in the area of Torbat-e-Haidari, near Mashad, and it was they, not the Baluch, who produced many of the rugs which, for the past fifty years or so, most collectors and writers have considered to be the finest and most archetypal products of the Baluch looms. Within the wider context of carpet studies, this might be considered an argument of fairly minor significance, but for specialists in east Iranian tribal weaving, it has the impact of a nuclear bomb.

I have to say, having read Mr Craycraft's thesis several times with great care, that I find his principal argument unconvincing, not least because of the fact that had it been the Karai – a tribe which not even Iranian specialists had previously considered to be significant weavers, or weavers at all – who had produced so famous a groups of rugs, their name would surely have cropped up before now, if only as a commercial label in the Iranian bazaars (although the market has not placed much value on such weavings until comparatively recently, they always seem to have been highly regarded by collectors and writers). I find it difficult to believe that, even in the main east Iranian bazaar at Mashad, these rugs would always have been described as Baluch if they were the work of another local tribe and one which, moreover, was apparently the most important in that area.

The distinctions in structure and design which Mr Craycraft uses to enforce his argument would be fine if there was one structure or one group of designs which could be said to be typically Baluch. But neither is the case and I do not understand why those characteristics which he chooses as significant pointers to a specifically Karai origin could not equally well be said to be indicative of a Baluch tribal origin in the Torbat-e-Haidari region, as I believe them to be. I once owned a rug identical to that illustrated by Mr Craycraft in plate 7 of his catalogue and I have also owned rugs of similar age, quality and design to his plates 1-4. Plate 7, however, although structurally indistinguishable on paper from the others, is a very different animal. My example was in full pile and had a handle and colour so different from the others that I fail to see how all five of the Adraskand rugs can be used as evidence of a common origin.

I have discussed the Adraskand catalogue at some length for three reasons; firstly it is an extremely interesting publication illustrating some superb rugs; secondly, whatever one might think of its principal thesis, it is a courageous attempt to add to our knowledge of, and bring order to, a very complex area of tribal weaving; and thirdly, it demonstrates how difficult it is to attribute accurately oriental rugs of even quite recent vintage.

Colonel Boucher, as any dedicated rug collector would, shows a deep awareness of the shifting nature of east Iranian rug attributions and has demonstrated a willingness to acknowledge new research in his catalogue by placing a significant number of his pieces (plates 52-65) in a category which he describes as 'Baluch in name only'. This gently ironic designation reveals the problematic nature of the subject. But I am equally convinced that at least some of the weavings placed in this latter category are as Baluch as anything else in the Colonel's collection.

So much for the problems, which have been deftly handled by Colonel Boucher in his description of each piece. He has generally acknowledged the existence of contradictory attributions, but has tended to keep to a narrow path, inviting others to deviate from it if they wish. I think he has been wise in this, for a distillation of all the various lines of research which have appeared in specialist publications over the last decade, the majority of which can be found in the bibliography, would probably have caused more confusion than clarification.

This leads me to a few brief comments on the collection itself and also on Colonel Boucher's catalogue. In his foreword, Barry Jacobs has rightly observed that this is a "collector's collection", an apparent tautology which is anything but. Just why not is neatly explained by Dr Jacobs in his opening and closing paragraphs, words which, in this age of art market madness, have an uncomfortable ring. Today, there are so many people with large amounts of money to spend on 'art' that true collecting, the slow obsessive search enlivened by passion and sensitivity, has been subsumed in a welter of vulgar accumulation or, equally despicable, mere 'autograph collecting'. But there will always be, one fervently hopes, the true collector, who is interested in neither fame, fortune nor the glamorous trappings of museum 'board membership' or gallery 'openings' (which in recent years have become almost as newsworthy as old-style Hollywood premières). The great collector is motivated simply by the search for beauty and will often find it in places where no-one had thought to look before.

It is immediately clear that this is a catalogue of one person's collection, a collection which, although excellent overall, shows those provocative quirks and predilections of taste which always enliven and make more fascinating groups of objects which have come together through the dedication and love of one individual. At the beginning of this preface I mentioned David Black and Clive Loveless, who have done as much as anyone to popularise tribal weaving in Europe and to convert people to their belief – now taken for granted – that the weavings of the nomadic and semi-nomadic tribes of Turkey, Iran, the Caucasus and Central Asia, although rarely pre-dating the 19th century (except in the case of Anatolia) and often from well into the 20th, are as worthy of serious consideration as the rugs of any other period.

In the United States much the same achievement may be attributed to three individuals who, although collectors rather than dealers, have taken the trouble to exhibit and publish catalogues of their own rugs and those of other like-minded collectors – Joseph V. McMullan, H. McCoy Jones and Jeff Boucher. My own career as a Baluch collector was prompted not only by the Black and Loveless catalogue but equally by the McCoy Jones and Boucher catalogue of Baluch rugs, published in 1974 under the auspices of the International Hajji Baba Society. Therefore, as far as my interest in Iranian tribal weaving is concerned, I look upon Jeff Boucher as one of my mentors. Despite the fact that my own Baluch collection has long since been dispersed (I am particularly happy to see that one or two pieces have ended up with the Colonel himself), and that my interest in Iranian weaving has taken a westward course, settling, for the time being, around the Chahar Mahall Valley, I still consider Jeff Boucher to be one of the greatest and most influential collectors of his generation. His invitation to write the preface for this long-awaited catalogue – the wait has been well worth it – is, therefore, one which I have been both delighted and honoured to accept.

Ian Bennett
London, May 1989

INTRODUCTION

"Think, in this batter'd Caravanserai
Whose portals are alternate Night and Day,
How Sultan after Sultan with his Pomp
Abode his destined Hour, and went his way."
— *The Rubaiyat of Omar Khayyam*

DEPARTED, LIKE THE SULTANS from this Caravanserai of Life, are the weavers of the rugs in this collection. Gone with them are the knowledge and skill which enabled the peasant and nomad to produce such masterpieces of tribal art. All are victims of advancing civilisation with its improved transportation and accompanying commercialism. Most Baluchi rugs woven today are in designs popular in the trade, with a pile of synthetically dyed wool loosely knotted on a base of mill-spun cotton and minus the often elaborately woven kilim ends so valued by collectors. However, the Aimaq in Afghanistan and the Baluchi of Sistan and Baluchistan still weave an all wool product in tribal designs, but the quality is low and the dyes used are largely chemical.

My interest in lovely old Baluchi rugs, woven in fine silky wool in the designs of their ancestors, dyed in soft natural colours, and crafted with the tender loving care that is evident in objects woven for the weaver's own use, was firmly established in 1974 when I was involved in the International Hajji Baba Society exhibition of Baluchi rugs held that year. I wanted to learn more about the Baluchi people and to build a collection of the most interesting rugs I could locate and acquire. Initially I would accept only what I considered a true Baluchi product, although I realised that other neighbouring tribes wove some rugs more or less in the Baluchi manner. However, as I became more knowledgeable, I began to appreciate outstanding related examples of the neighbouring weavers and thus began to collect some of their products as well. These are included in Part II of the plates while Baluchi examples are shown in Part I. Thus, in this work I have included rare and/or outstanding examples of Baluchi weavings which have fascinated me, and have published them in the hope that they will bring pleasure and inspiration to others interested in those tribal weavings of the past which will soon be available for study only in museums and a few specialised collections.

Jeff W. Boucher
Alexandria, Virginia

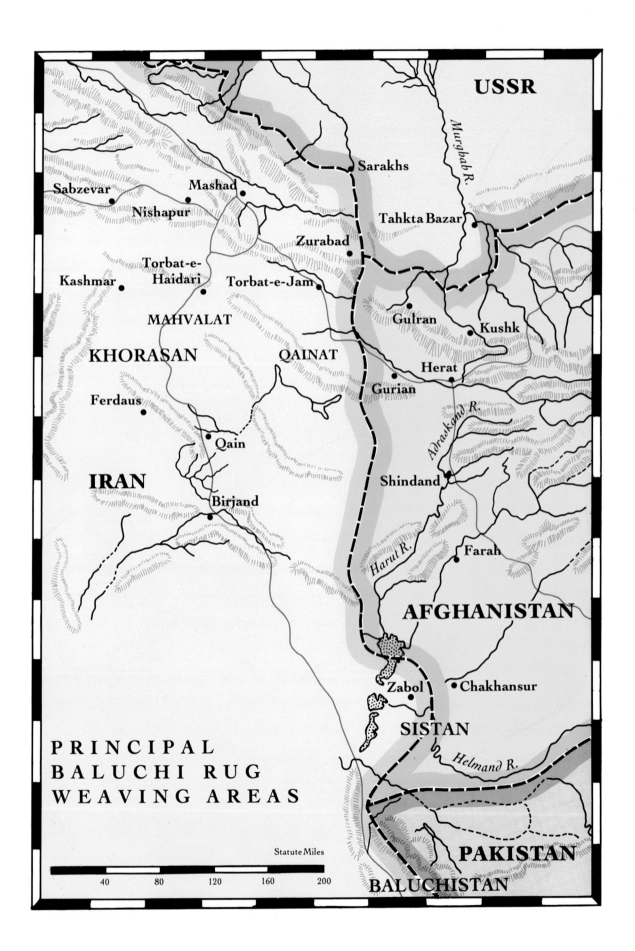

PRINCIPAL
BALUCHI RUG
WEAVING AREAS

Statute Miles

40   80   120   160   200

BALUCHI HISTORY

IT IS WELL-KNOWN that very little authentic information has been established regarding the origin of the great tribes of the Middle East and Central Asia. The Baluchis are no exception. They were almost completely illiterate and their centuries' long migratory existence, their exposure to wars, to banditry and to enslavement, prevented records being made and safeguarded.

The earliest references to the Baluchi appear to be those contained in Persian literature. Thus, Longworth Dames in the *Encyclopaedia of Islam* (1913) states that Baloc (Baluchi) seems to be an old Persian word meaning cockscomb or crest (Firdawsi describes them as wearing such crests) and that their early location seems to have been near the Persian shores of the Caspian Sea, where Nawshirwan made war against them.

Baluchi legends suggest that they originated in Arabia or Arabian areas such as Syria; but more probably they are a mixture of several races of northern origin in the desert lands within the confines of ancient Persia. Linguistic arguments put forward by Dr R.W. Frye in 1961 support this theory. It appears that they were driven from the Caspian area by the earliest invasions from Central Asia, into the Kirman area where they were reported by Arab geographers of the 11th and 12th centuries. The Seljuk conquest of Kirman in 1037 and the Mongol invasion of 1219 pushed them further to the east, where they subsequently spread throughout Baluchistan and northward into western Afghanistan and eastern Persia. There are several conflicting accounts of the movement of the Baluchis into Khorasan Province. The most likely story of a major movement is that Nadir Shah moved a group into this area from Baluchistan to form a barrier against marauding Turkoman tribes, and that others followed later, toward the end of the 19th century, due to famine conditions in the south. In Afghanistan, the Baluchis are found principally in the Sistan area of Nimruz Province, but small groups are also found north towards the Soviet border.

Today the Baluchis, who are mostly Sunni Moslems, number about 15,000 in the Soviet Socialist Republic of Turkmenistan, 500,000 in Iran and 70,000 in Afghanistan. The remainder, amounting to perhaps 800,000, form the majority of the population of Baluchistan Province in Pakistan. In Sistan, Baluchistan and Afghanistan, the Baluchi are mainly nomadic or semi-nomadic; in northern Khorasan they are partly nomadic but many have long been sedentary and live in villages. Despite increased efforts for improvement by their various governments, they remain one of the poorest and least advanced peoples in all three countries.

THE WEAVERS

Only a small portion of the Baluchi population weave rugs. Currently, women and girls in Baluchi groups living in the Sistan area and northward in Khorasan to Sarakhs account for most of the production of pile rugs. The tribes of Baluchistan weave only flat-woven items and a few pile items, primarily for their own use. These are generally unattractive, loosely woven, of very poor and dull colours, and are rarely seen outside the areas where they are made.

The greatest Persian production, as well as the highest sustained weaving quality, comes from the Torbat-e-Haidari, Torbat-e-Jam, Nishapur and Sarakhs areas of Khorasan and from the vicinity of Zabol in Sistan to the south. Nearly all of these rugs are shipped to Mashad for marketing.

According to A. Cecil Edwards, the principal weaving tribes of Khorasan at the time of his study were the Bahluli in the Torbat-e-Haidari districts of Khaf and Djangal; the Baizidi in the Mahvalat district of Torbat-e-Haidari and in Qain; the Kolah-derazi in Torbat-e-Haidari and in Kashmar; the Jan Mirzai in Zaveh and the Ali-Ek in Torbat-e-Haidari; the Rahim Khani in Torbat-e-Haidari and Sarakhs; the Brahui in Torbat-e-Haidari and Sarakhs; the Kurkheilli (Salar Khani) in Torbat-e-Haidari and Jangal; the Hassanzai in several areas; and the Jan Begi in Roshkar (Torbat-e-Haidari).

The Bahluri in Persia, listed by Edwards as Baluchi, are probably of Turkic origin, but they have long been considered as Baluchi and are therefore listed as such in this study.

There are many other Baluchi tribes and sub-tribes which weave rugs in the general area mentioned above. No attempt will be made to name them all here as such an accurate accounting of contemporary weavers would be beyond the scope of this study. In addition, there are other well-known groups, who are not Baluchi, but who weave rugs resembling Baluchi products in this area. In Persia the most important are the Timuris of the Torbat-e-Jam and Zurabad areas, the Quchan Kurds, and the Firadows Arabs. In western Afghanistan, according to Alfred Janata, the Aimaq, a Farsi speaking Sunni people of some five hundred clan names weave the rugs known until recently as 'Herat' and 'Adraskand' Baluchi. The best quality weaving can be assigned to about forty Timuri clans, approximately twelve of which live in northeastern Persia as well as northwestern Afghanistan. Two of the best-known clans of this latter group are the Yaqub-Khani of the Zurabad area and the Dokhtar-e-Ghazi of northwest Afghanistan. Some clans categorised as Aimaq also include persons of Turkic, Persian, Mongol and Arab extraction, which could account for some of their weavings being Turkish as well as Persian knotted.

THE RUGS

The most obvious method of recognising an old Baluchi rug is by its colour and to a lesser extent by its design. The colours used were basically blue, red, brown and black – highlighted with small amounts of ivory – which generally produced a dark effect. Camel-coloured grounds were sometimes used, often in prayer rugs, but the most common ground colour for Persian Baluchi rugs was dark blue, while Afghanistan Aimaq weavers used more brown. Most modern rugs are apt to contain bright, synthetic dyes and thus bear little resemblance to their earlier ancestors. In size, the rugs are mostly small, two to five by three to nine feet, since they were woven under primitive conditions on horizontal looms. Most old Baluchi rugs are all wool, Persian knotted, double-wefted and have long kilim bands or aprons at both ends. With few exceptions they have a selvage of black or dark brown goat hair, which is also sometimes mixed in the warp. Many modern rugs have a cotton foundation and most omit the colourful kilim apron at the ends.

It is much more difficult to attribute old Baluchi rugs to a certain tribe or sub-tribe than the rugs of most other weavers. The reasons for this are that the Baluchis live in remote and isolated areas; in the past they were largely nomadic and many are nomadic to semi-nomadic today; their numerous tribal and sub-tribal names are continually changing and popular Baluchi designs are now often woven by weavers of different tribes as modern transportation has increased their knowledge of market trends. A 20th century weaver of a certain design is not always therefore the descendent of the 19th century tribe to which the design belonged.

This problem in attribution is reflected in the rug descriptions accompanying the plates in this publication. In most cases available information will support only an area of probable production rather than the name of the weaver's tribe. There are some exceptions, however, particularly with reference to certain areas where rugs with marked characteristics have been woven by several tribes and sub-tribes for generations. The Torbat-e-Haidari area of northeast Khorasan, for instance, where some of the finest Baluchi rugs — called 'Mashad Baluchi' in the trade – have long been woven. These were primarily woven in dark blues, reds and browns, outlined in black or small amounts of white, which produce a blueish-red or purple sheen when light strikes the fine glossy wool. All the old rugs had very handsome kilim ends, often elaborately decorated in weft-float technique. General Bogoliouboff purchased a rug of this type there around 1900 and published a colour plate of it in his famous book, *Tapis de L'Asie Centrale*. An examination of this plate will greatly assist one in identifying rugs woven in this area today.

SYNTHETIC DYES

Due to their nomadic or semi-nomadic existence and the remoteness of their bleak and uninviting land, the blight of commercialism reached the Baluchis later than weavers in most areas of the Middle East. However, when the industrial dye fuchsine arrived in eastern Persia in approximately 1880, the illiterate Baluchi weavers were fascinated. Here was the opportunity to incorporate colours into their weavings that were beyond the scope of natural dyes. Many outstanding woven items made for a dowry or as presentation pieces for important people were therefore highlighted with one or more of the new dyes, as in plates 19, 28 and 29.

DESIGNS

Many oriental rug writers consider the Baluchi weavers to be copyists with no designs which are entirely their own. A study of the rugs woven by these talented weavers does not corroborate this claim. Some designs were no doubt copied, but they usually show a decided Baluchi rendition and some are woven only by Baluchi weavers. A few examples of the latter follow.

The Baluchi tree-of-life design is unique and different from all others, as seen in plates 1, 2, 24, 32, 38 and 39.

The cockscomb or crest motif as seen in the border designs of plates 8 and 36.

The animal-tree design of plates 33, 34, 35 and 58. The Baluchis, as well as early Turkish weavers, may have acquired this design during ancient contacts with Turkic steppe nomads, as noted in the description of plate 58, but it is entirely possible that the Baluchis of the Caspian Sea area were the first to weave this motif.

The tile pattern of plate 45 with four elongated hexagons enclosing 'S' forms.

The peacock design which fills the field of plates 12, 48 and 61. Other weavers weave bird designs, but not in this manner.

The repeating leaf and floral stem motif in the border design of plates 48 and 58.

The vine meander with floral pennants design in the borders of the bag faces in plates 33, 34 and 35.

Finally, there is an infinite number of combinations of motifs shared by other weavers into an overall design which is truly Baluchi.

This alone seems to qualify the Baluchi weaver as a creative artist rather than as a simple copyist.

OTHER WOVEN ITEMS

During the period when these rugs were woven, the Baluchi wove many objects for their own use other than rugs. Examples of some of these included in this collection are listed as follows:

Saddle Bag (Khorjin). These bags are made in many sizes but all consist of two halves bound together at the top by a woven strip or bridge. The bags in this collection have pile-woven faces for each half with a flat-woven back. They are woven on a flat loom with a single warp thread; first one piled face, then its back, then the bridge, then the second back, and last the second piled face. When the weaving is completed the faces are folded up to the bridge and the sides closed. When in use they are thrown over the back of a pack animal with a half to either side (plates 56, 58 and 63, also plate 48, which shows a bag face with the back removed).

Salt Bag (Namakdam). This is a small bottle-shaped bag with a narrow neck at the top. The primary use of these bags is to contain salt, but spoons, dried fruit and other prized items may be stored in this container (plate 29).

Sofreh. In general, sofrehs are rectangular flat-woven rugs which are spread on the floor at mealtime and serve as table-cloths. Fine sofrehs are used only when entertaining guests. They have richly decorated kilim ends and some have pile borders (plates 30 and 31).

Ru-Korssi. On cold nights the Baluchi use a small square table (*korssi*) to cover the *mangal*, a metal or clay dish, containing glowing hot charcoal. This table is then covered with felts or blankets and the nomads sit around this with their hands or feet under the blanket to keep warm. At night they sleep on rugs with their feet under this blanket. On such occasions an elaborately decorated, small, square, flat-woven rug, the ru-korssi, is placed on top of the blankets. The ru-korssi may also be used to cover the table when it is not in the heating process. If special guests arrive and food is served, the ru-korssi often serves as a sofreh (plates 13, 25, 26, 27 and 28).

Pillow (Balisht). This is a small narrow bag with a pile-woven front which is filled with down or cotton and the open end closed. The bag is then used as a head pillow (plates 16 and 32).

Pillow (Poshti). A small square bag with a pile-woven front which, as in the preceding case, is filled with down or cotton and the open end closed. It is then used as a back pillow or cushion (plate 36).

Storage Bags. Rectangular bags with slits and closure loops at one end are made for use as storage containers, but can be used as pillows or cushions as required (plates 42, 43 and 49).

Saddle Rug. A small rug that is normally placed on the saddle for decoration and comfort to the rider (plate 15).

Vanity Bag. A small bag approximately one foot square used to carry razors, combs and other toilet articles. All are flat-woven in Baluchistan, but northward they are sometimes woven in pile. Most are elaborately decorated with tassels, beads or shells (plate 50).

THE PLATES
PART I

BALUCHI WEAVINGS
PLATES 1-51

PLATE 1

BALUCHI PRAYER RUG, JAN BEGI,
Northeast Persia, Khorasan, Torbat-e-Haidari,
mid 19th century.
2'5" × 4'4".

A SLENDER, STYLIZED TREE-OF-LIFE with branches in full leaf dominates the camel hair field of the mihrab, while similar motifs fill the camel ground of each spandrel. Beautifully executed large bands of ruby-red and dark blue weft-float decorate the kilim ends of the piece. This high standard of workmanship is also evident in the five borders, four guard stripes, and the dainty reciprocal trefoil or *medachyl* inner stripe which separates the field from the main borders. Finally, all voids in the field are filled with eight-pointed stars and clever cruciform motifs. Every detail of this rug indicates that it was woven by a masterweaver who spared no effort to create a fine rug.

TECHNICAL ANALYSIS
Warp: Z2S, ivory wool, alternate warps slightly depressed.
Weft: 2Z, two shoots brown wool.
Pile: 2Z, wool and camel hair, Persian knot open to left, 144 knots per sq.. in.
Selvage: Not original.
Ends: Striped plain-weave with three inch bands of weft-float and twined guard stripes.
Colours: Ruby-red (cochineal), coral-red, violet-brown, light brown (corroded), natural
    camel, dark blue, surmey (blue-black), and ivory (bleached).

PLATE 2

BALUCHI PRAYER RUG,
Northeast Persia, Khorasan, Torbat-e-Haidari,
late 19th century.
2′9″ × 5′0″.

IT IS INTERESTING TO NOTE the changes in these lovely prayer rugs with the tree-of-life motif filling the natural camel ground of the mihrab as we come to the late 19th century. This rug has two striking features which mark it as unusual. i) The wine-red central border decorated with dark blue and ivory floral forms frames the field, but the top portion does not follow the contours of the prayer arch as is usual. ii) The small camel-ground panels at each side of the prayer arch contain the inscription "There is no God but Allah and Mohammed is his prophet". Within the arch, a red and blue frame encloses a camel ground containing what appears to be the outline of a mosque with a minaret at the top right and a dome at the left. A hanging lamp is suspended from the top of the interior. Simulated rays of light project from the outer perimeter of the frame – green (a holy colour) from the top and gold for the remainder. The two guard borders contain the 'horse's tail' motif which became popular in Baluchi weaving during this period. All design elements are outlined in light brown wool. The piece is well woven in soft, lustrous wool.

TECHNICAL ANALYSIS
Warp: Z2S, ivory wool, level back.
Weft: 2Z, two, occasionally three, shoots brown wool.
Pile: 2Z, wool, silk and camel hair, Persian knot open to left. 108 knots per sq. in.
Selvage: Four cables, (Z2S)3Z, wrapped in dark brown goat hair.
Ends: Striped plain-weave kilim with half inch band of weft-float.
Colours: Light coral-red, light wine-red, dark blue, natural camel, light brown, dark brown, apple-green (silk), gold (silk), and ivory (bleached wool).

PLATE 3

BALUCHI RUG,
Northeast Persia, Khorasan, Torbat-e-Haidari area,
mid 19th century.
3'4" × 4'9".

THE VARIEGATED LIGHT RED to deep purple-red field of this small rug contains horizontal rows of blue and dark brown long-petalled rosettes separated by smaller ivory eight-petalled *Mina Khani* variant flower heads. Throughout the field, voids in the design are filled with tree, flower and plant forms in the popular Baluchi manner. The light red major border contains a repeat of a split tendril form and a small rosette with a central cruciform motif. These forms are separated by half-diamond shapes projecting inward from the border. A slender reciprocal ivory and surmey vine and 'V' leaf outer border frames the piece, and an attractive barber pole inner border in the colours of the field has small ivory dots as colour separations. A rare rug with early design features.

TECHNICAL ANALYSIS
Warp: Z2S, ivory wool, level back.
Weft: 2Z, two shoots light brown wool.
Pile: 2Z, wool, Persian knot open to left, 99 knots per sq. in.
Selvage: Two cables of two warps each wrapped in dark brown goat hair.
Ends: Six and a half inches flat-weave in plain, interlocked and weft-float kilim.
Colours: Light red, dark purple-red, blue-green, mid blue, dark blue, dark brown, surmey (blue-black) and ivory.

PLATE 4

BALUCHI RUG, BAIZIDI,
Northeast Persia, Khorasan, Torbat-e-Haidari, Mahvalat area,
circa 1870.
3'3" × 5'6".

A LATTICE OF THIN RED LINES with small ivory flower heads at connecting points divides the dark blue field into diamond shaped openings, each containing a flower head with a central eight-pointed star. The striking, clear red major border is decorated with a finely designed meandering vine containing clusters of three ivory *Mina Khani* flowers alternating with a dark blue rosette. The dark olive-green wool used in some of the flower heads is corroded and worn low, giving a carved effect. This rug was lovingly cared for by its previous owner, as is apparent from its near perfect condition, including the preservation of the knotted warp ends, despite the age of the piece. Woven in fine lustrous wool.

TECHNICAL ANALYSIS
Warp: Z2S, ivory wool, alternate warps slightly depressed.
Weft: 2Z, two shoots dark brown wool.
Pile: 2Z, wool, Persian knot open to left, 120 knots per sq. in.
Selvage: Four cables, Z4S, wrapped in dark brown goat hair.
Ends: Top six inches and bottom seven inches in plain-weave kilim with a two and a half inch interlocked, deep-toothed panel bounded by quarter inch ivory weft-float stripes. This is followed by a one inch band in soumak technique, and a one inch ivory plain-woven band containing a line of horizontal 'S' figures.
Colours: Clear light red, brown-red, violet-brown, dark olive-green (corroded), dark blue, dark brown, and ivory.
Provenance: From the estate of Richard Halliburton, world traveller, author and lecturer, who was lost in the Pacific Ocean during a violent typhoon in 1939 while en route from Hong Kong to San Francisco on a Chinese junk.

PLATE 5

BALUCHI RUG, BAIZIDI,
Northeast Persia, Khorasan, Torbat-e-Haidari, Mahvalat area,
circa 1875.
3′6″ × 6′9″.

THIS RUG IS WOVEN IN FINE SOFT WOOL with the dark blue field popular among Torbat-e-Haidari weavers, and a clear red major border decorated with *Mina Khani* flowers as woven in the Mahvalat area. The double-stripe lattice divides the field into diamond openings, each containing a flower head with a central eight-pointed star. The central flower head is highlighted by an ivory star. Connecting points in the lattice are similarly highlighted by four small ivory flower heads. A lovely rug woven in the finest Baluchi tradition.

TECHNICAL ANALYSIS
Warp: Z2S, ivory wool, alternate warps slightly depressed.
Weft: 2Z, two shoots brown wool.
Pile: 2Z, wool, Persian knot open to left, 111 knots per sq. in.
Selvage: Four cables, Z4S, wrapped in dark brown goat hair.
Ends: Seven inch plain-weave kilim with a two and a half inch interlocked, deep-toothed panel bounded by quarter inch ivory weft-float stripes and terminating in a one inch band in soumak technique.
Colours: Clear light red, coral-red, brown-red, dark blue, dark brown, and ivory.

PLATE 6

BALUCHI RUG,
Northeast Persia, Khorasan, Torbat-e-Haidari, Mahvalat area,
circa 1875.
3'8" × 6'4".

THE FINE SILKY WOOL and clear colours of the best Baluchi pieces have been used. A lattice divides the field into diagonal rows of diamond shaped panels containing stylized flower heads. The black pile outlining the red flower heads is reduced by corrosion, which produces a carved effect. When strong light strikes the light blue flower heads they appear to scintillate in a fascinating way. The ivory flowers stand out against the red major border in this rendition of the *Mina Khani* design. The selvages have a rippling condition resulting from uneven shrinkage in the rug when washed (the horse hair cables of the selvages did not shrink, leaving them slightly longer than the rug). The two small animals placed in the major border opposite each lower corner of the field add interest to the piece.

TECHNICAL ANALYSIS

Warp: Z2S, ivory wool, level back.
Weft: 2Z, two shoots brown wool.
Pile: 2Z, wool, Persian knot open to right, 80 knots per sq. in.
Selvage: Four large horse hair cables, Z8S, wrapped in dark brown goat hair.
Ends: Two inch plain, striped kilim with weft-float decoration.
Colours: Clear light red, light blue, dark blue, violet-brown, dark brown, black (corroded), and ivory.
Published: Yoruk: The Nomadic Weaving Tradition of the Middle East, editor Anthony N. Landreau, Pittsburg 1978, no. 104.
Provenance: From a London collection of Baluchi rugs formed in the last half of the 19th century.

PLATE 7

BALUCHI RUG,
Northeast Persia, Khorasan, Torbat-e-Haidari,
late 19th century.
3'0" × 7'0".

A RED DOUBLE-LINE LATTICE with four flower connectors divides the dark blue field into diamond openings, each containing a flower head with a central eight-pointed star. The star in the central coral-red flower head is woven in magenta and gold silk. Some of the stars in the upper half of the field are similarly highlighted with silk. The major border is filled with a chain of light red hexagons with split tendrils projecting from each end and a brown-red centre containing an attractive flower head. This motif is not common and may be an old Baluchi design almost lost by the last quarter of the 19th century. Probably the most attractive part of the entire design is the striking red and light blue vine and leaf meander in the outer minor border. This rug, woven in fine lustrous wool, was no doubt some Baluchi weaver's proud creation.

TECHNICAL ANALYSIS

Warp; Z2S, ivory wool, alternate warps slightly depressed.

Weft: 2Z, two shoots brown wool.

Pile: 2Z, wool and silk, Persian knot open to left, 100 knots per sq. in.

Selvage: Two cables, Z6S, originally wrapped in dark brown goat hair but now
　　mostly missing.

Ends: Four and a half inch plain-weave striped kilim with one inch interlocked barber
　　pole panel.

Colours: Light red, coral-red, brown-red, light blue, dark blue, dark blue-green, dark olive-
　　green (corroded), magenta and gold silk, and ivory.

PLATE 8

BALUCHI RUG,
Northeast Persia, Khorasan, Torbat-e-Haidari area,
circa 1870.
3'7" × 6'2".

THE VARIEGATED VIOLET-BROWN FIELD of this rare rug is
entirely composed of three panels of the popular major border design
known as the 'Turkoman line' rendered in light blue, dark blue and light
cherry-red. The violet-brown major border is decorated with a chain of
unique, elongated blue hexagon motifs with ivory spearheads projecting
inward from the vertical sides. Attractive light cherry-red minor borders
contain 'S' repeats resembling cocks – the Baluchi symbol of authority or
leadership. The pile is lustrous and in good condition in most places, but in
certain areas the dark violet-brown ground and black outlines show the
corrosive effect of the dyes.

TECHNICAL ANALYSIS
Warp: Z2S, ivory wool, level back.
Weft: 2Z, two, sometimes three, shoots brown wool.
Pile: 2Z, wool, Persian knot open to left, 126 knots per sq. in.
Selvage: Two cables of ivory wool warp (Z2S)6Z wrapped in dark brown goat hair.
Ends: Five inch plain, interlocked kilim with bands of soumak brocade.
Colours: Light cherry-red, wine-red, light blue, dark blue, violet-brown (partly corroded),
black (corroded), and ivory.
Published: *The Persian Carpet* by Lefevre & Partners, London 1977, plate 38.

PLATE 9

BALUCHI RUG,
Northeast Persia, Khorasan, Torbat-e-Haidari area,
circa 1880.
4'3" × 6'3".

AN OVERALL LATTICE DESIGN connected at each intersection by an attractive five-spot dice motif decorates the field of this piece. The dark red major border contains the familiar 'Turkoman line' design so popular with Baluchi weavers. The equally popular ivory 'ocean wave' minor borders are augmented by the addition of a red or blue triangle in the wave base. The elaborate kilim aprons are best represented at the bottom of the rug where an eight inch band remains.

TECHNICAL ANALYSIS

Warp: Z2S, ivory wool, alternate warps slightly depressed.
Weft: 2Z, two, sometimes three, shoots dark brown wool.
Pile: 2Z, wool, Persian knot open to left, 80 knots per sq. in.
Selvage: Four cables, (Z2S)3Z, each wrapped in dark brown goat hair.
Ends: Top – three and a half inch (reduced), plain and interlocked kilim with a weft-float stripe; bottom – eight inch plain striped and interlocked kilim with three bands of weft-float.
Colours: Clear light red, dark red, light blue, mid-blue, dark brown (corroded), and ivory.

PLATE 10

BALUCHI RUG,
Northeast Persia, Khorasan, Torbat-e-Haidari,
circa 1875.
3'2" × 5'0".

A RARE RUG with the allover boteh design on an ivory ground. The serrated long-necked boteh with the split trunk base is intriguing and appears more floral than the normal boteh motif. Most known examples with this design are prayer rugs of the 20th century. The simple major border with alternating dark blue eight-pointed stars and rectangular figures with floral buds projecting from the sides is most interesting. Also note the three small upside-down animals — one without a head – which appear in the lower left hand corner of the field.

TECHNICAL ANALYSIS
Warp: Z2S, ivory wool, level back.
Weft: 2Z, two shoots brown wool.
Pile: 2Z, wool, Persian knot open to left, 96 knots per sq. in.
Selvage: Two cables, Z4S, wrapped in dark brown goat-hair.
Ends: Plain, interlocked kilim with two bands in weft-float technique.
Colours: Light and medium red, medium brown (corroded), dark brown, dark blue, and ivory.
Literature: A closely related example appears in *Rare Oriental Carpets VIII* by Eberhart Herrmann, Munich 1986, plate 98.

PLATE 11

BALUCHI RUG,
Northeast Persia, Khorasan, Torbat-e-Haidari area,
circa 1880.
3'9" × 6'3".

THE DARK BLUE FIELD of this fascinating rug is decorated with
fourteen different multicoloured gül types, irregularly placed throughout
the field with all voids in-between filled with small stylized floral rosettes,
stars, and geometric forms creating a riot of colour. But the two most
outstanding design features of this piece are the magnificent clear light red
major border containing an exceptionally fine rendition of the popular
'Turkoman line' and the small, apricot double-cruciform motif placed in
each corner of the field.

TECHNICAL ANALYSIS

Warp: Z2S, ivory wool, alternate warps deeply depressed.
Weft: 2Z, two shoots dark brown wool.
Pile: 2Z, wool, Persian knot open to left, 108 knots per sq. in.
Selvage: Eight cables, (Z2S)2Z, wrapped in dark brown goat hair.
Ends: Five inch striped, plain-woven kilim with a central band of ivory weft-float.
Colours: Clear light red, pinkish-red, brown-red, light and dark brown (corroded), apricot,
    dark blue, and ivory.

PLATE 12

BALUCHI RUG,
Northeast Persia, Khorasan, Torbat-e-Haidari area,
late 19th century.
2′4″ × 4′3″.

THIS SOPHISTICATED LITTLE RUG with allover red and ivory peacocks in diagonal rows on a dark blue ground with a mid blue abrash is typical of a dowry or presentation piece from the Torbat-e-Haidari area. This attribution is further borne out by the fine weave of the piece and the delicate workmanship of the wide band, woven in deep-toothed panels of red and blue bounded by chains of dainty ivory flower heads in the kilim ends. The crown of the central bird in the lower ivory row is woven in silk, which prompted a former owner to refer to it as *"primus inter pares"*, or first among equals.

TECHNICAL ANALYSIS

Warp: Z2S, ivory wool, alternate warps moderately depressed.
Weft: 2Z, two shoots dark brown wool.
Pile: 2Z, wool and silk, Persian knot open to left, 99 knots per sq. in.
Selvage: Two cables, ivory wool, (Z2S)6Z, wrapped in dark brown wool.
Ends: Three and a half inch (reduced) plain interlocked kilim with outer band of half inch red, horizontal 'Z' forms in weft-float and two eighth inch chains of ivory flower heads in weft-float.
Colours: Brick-red, brown-red, mid-blue, dark blue, dark brown, black (corroded), light green (silk), and ivory.
Published: Rare Oriental Carpets VI by Eberhart Herrmann, Munich 1984, plate 75; *HALI* 34, 1987, p. 19.

PLATE 13

BALUCHI RU-KORSSI,
Northeast Persia, Khorasan, Torbat-e-Haidari area,
late 19th century.
4'2" × 4'2".

A SQUARE TABLE COVER with a light red, plain-weave field, in this instance decorated with five small dark blue and ivory hooked diamond forms rendered in weft-float technique. Dark blue interlocked serrated triangles with several small red and ivory flower heads project from the sides of the field, while smaller blue weft-float triangles are placed at the top of the field and small dark brown weft-float triangles are placed at the bottom. An attractive thin red stripe with ivory 'S' forms in weft-float appears at the base of the small triangles at both the top and bottom of the field. The dark blue pile major border is decorated with a continuous orange-red repeat of hexagons with projecting tendrils at either end and a purple-red centre which encloses an ivory floral rosette, similar to plate 7.

TECHNICAL ANALYSIS
Warp: Z2S, ivory wool, alternate warps slightly depressed. Kilim — fourteen warps per linear inch.
Weft: Z2, two shoots dark brown wool.
Pile: Z2, wool, Persian knot open to left, 98 knots per linear inch.
Selvage: Four cables, (Z2S)4Z, ivory wool wrapped in dark brown goat hair.
Ends: Plain-weave striped and interlocked kilim with band of weft-float bounded by double running-stitch guards.
Colours: Light red, orange-red, purple-red, light brown, violet-brown, dark brown, dark blue, and ivory.
Published: Baluchi Rugs by Jeff Boucher and H. McCoy Jones, Washington D.C. 1974, no. 33.

PLATE 14

BALUCHI TENT BAG,
Northeast Persia, Khorasan, Torbat-e-Haidari area,
mid 19th century.
2'4" × 2'6".

A HEXAGONAL LATTICE enclosing seven vertical rows of red hooked güls on a dark blue ground with a central ivory Memling gül containing a dark blue eight-pointed star fills the field. Open spaces are filled with red stars and small floral forms. The red primary border is decorated with a repeating pair of diagonal reciprocal wave and leaf forms while the secondary borders are composed of blue and red reciprocal wave forms with a small ivory cross motif at the base of each blue wave. Blue and red barber pole stripes separate the borders. An outstanding example, finely knotted in soft, silky wool.

TECHNICAL ANALYSIS
Warp: Z2S, ivory wool, level back.
Weft: 2Z, two shoots brown wool.
Pile: 2Z, wool, Persian knot open to left, 192 knots per sq. in.
Selvage: Two cables, Z8S, wrapped in brown wool. Sides closed by dark brown goat hair in a
    raised fish-bone stitch (mostly missing).
Ends: Top – plain-weave slit-tapestry with two one inch bands of weft-float and dark brown
    goat hair loops. End is folded and oversewn; bottom – plain-weave with one inch band of
    weft-float.
Colours: Copper-red, brick-red, dark blue, black (corroded), and ivory.

PLATE 15

BALUCHI SADDLE RUG, SALAR-KHANI,
Northeast Persia, Khorasan, Torbat-e-Haidari area,
circa 1870.
2'0" × 2'2".

SEVERAL GEOMETRIC AND FLORAL FORMS common to weavings of the Salar-Khani Baluchi are contained within the dark blue field. Prominent examples are the half stepped medallions protruding inward from the top and bottom of the field and the four feather, or leaf, forms with arrows pointing outward from the central diamond medallion. Dr Dietrich Wegner says this Herati design is called *keshmiri* by the Baluchi. Note that an unusual number of eight borders frames the central field. A finely woven old piece containing excellent wool and natural dyes. Truly the prized possession of some tribal leader.

TECHNICAL ANALYSIS
Warp: Z2S, ivory wool, level back.
Weft: 2Z, two, occasionally one, shoots brown wool.
Pile: 2Z, wool, Persian knot open to left, 150 knots per sq. in.
Selvage: Two cables, (Z2S)3&4Z, wrapped in rust-red wool.
Ends: Missing.
Colours: Light rust-red, dark blue, gold, violet-brown, black (corroded), and ivory.

PLATE 16

BALUCHI PILLOW (BALISHT), JAN BEGI,
Northeast Persia, Khorasan, Torbat-e-Haidari, Khaf Valley area,
late 19th century.
1'7" × 2'8".

AN ATTRACTIVE PILLOW with a central crowned tree having opposing birds' head leaves superimposed upon the camel field. At either side the weaver has placed a vertical row of serrated long-necked botehs each containing an eight-pointed star. Small floral plant devices, human (probably a family) and animal figures fill the voids in the field. The light red major border contains what appears to be a crude rendition of the Caucasian vine and wine glass motif.

TECHNICAL ANALYSIS
Warp: Z2S, ivory wool, alternate warps depressed 45°.
Weft: Z2, two shoots dark brown wool.
Pile: Z2, wool, Persian knot open to left, 111 knots per sq. in.
Selvage: Two cables of two warps each. Sides closed by dark brown goat hair in a raised fish-
  bone stitch (mostly missing).
Ends: A half inch plain-weave kilim with central chain-stitch strip in dark brown goat hair.
  The warp ends are turned under and sewn down.
Colours: Light red, brown-red, mid blue, dark blue, dark brown, camel and ivory.

PLATE 17

BALUCHI RUG, SULTAN-KHANI,
Northeast Persia, Khorasan, Kashmar area, vicinity of Kuh-e-Khab,
circa 1870.
3'0" × 6'3".

THIS LOVELY OLD RUG'S dark blue ground is covered with a brown-red lattice with diamond openings containing ivory, red and brown-red flower heads. The red flowers have alternating gold and ivory centres. The elongated ivory petals of this rendition of the familiar *Mina Khani* motif identifies the piece as Sultan-Khani weaving (Wegner, 1980, p. 90). The striking wide red major border contains a brown-red and dark blue vine meander with latchhook leaves and stylized flowers highlighted with gold and ivory centres. An interesting mid blue has been added at random in the plant forms throughout the border pattern. The secondary borders are composed of reciprocal dark brown and ivory 'ocean wave' forms. Blue and red barber pole stripes separate the borders. Note the gold in the lower portion of the outer stripe. The piece is woven in soft, lustrous wool.

TECHNICAL ANALYSIS
Warp: Z2S, ivory wool, alternate warps depressed 45°.
Weft: 2Z, two shoots dark brown wool.
Pile: 2Z, wool, Persian knot open to left, 80 knots per sq. in.
Selvage: Four cables, (Z2S)4Z, wrapped in dark brown goat hair. Outside cable repaired in
    dark brown wool.
Ends: Top – six inch striped plain-weave with two inch interlocked chevron panel and two
    bands of weft-float; bottom – four inch striped plain-weave with two bands of weft-float.
Colours: Red, brown-red, medium blue, dark blue, dark brown, gold and ivory.
Published: Baluchi Rugs by Jeff Boucher and H. McCoy Jones, Washington D.C. 1974,
    plate 13.

PLATE 18.

BALUCHI RUG, SULTAN-KHANI,
Northeast Persia, Khorasan, Kashmar area, vicinity of Kuh-e-Khab,
early 20th century.
4'6" × 7'6".

CHERRY-RED AND MAHOGANY-RED VINES, floral rosettes and
ivory *Mina Khani* flowers are contained within the dark blue field. The
cherry-red major border is filled with vines, flowers and floral rosettes in
the colours of the field, while the minor borders are rendered in an ivory
and surmey reciprocal 'ocean wave' design. The rug has a thick, velvety
handle indicative of its fine wool and depressed warp construction.

TECHNICAL ANALYSIS
Warp: Z2S, ivory wool, alternate warps deeply depressed.
Weft: 2Z, two shoots dark brown wool.
Pile: 2Z, wool, Persian knot open to right, 96 knots per sq. in.
Selvage: Four cables, Z6S, wrapped with dark brown goat hair.
Ends: Missing.
Colours: Cherry-red, mahogany-red, dark brown, surmey (blue-black), dark blue, and ivory.

PLATE 19

BALUCHI RUG,
Northeast Persia, Khorasan, Kashmar area,
circa 1880.
3'6" × 5'11".

BALUCHI RUGS IN THE MINA KHANI DESIGN, of the comparatively early period of this handsome example, reveal the rich depth of colour and alluring surface patina which are unique to rugs of this type and origin, making them among the most widely admired and sought after of the tribe's weavings. This example shows the stimulating design interaction between field and border, excellently set off by the ivory 'ocean wave' guard borders, which also serve to place the central pattern stress on the six-petalled ivory rosettes of the field. A few touches of fuchsine-dyed silk help in dating the work to the last twenty years of the 19th century and underline the particular merit placed on the rug by its weaver.

TECHNICAL ANALYSIS
Warp: Z2S, ivory wool, alternate warps deeply depressed.
Weft: 2Z, two, sometimes three, shoots dark brown wool.
Pile: 2Z, wool and silk, Persian knot open to left, 63 knots per sq. in.
Selvage: Four cables of dark brown horse hair, wrapped in dark brown goat hair. Extensively
    repaired in dark brown wool.
Ends: Plain-weave striped and interlocked kilim.
Colours: Cherry-red, light blue, mid-blue, dark brown, black, violet-brown, tip-faded
    fuchsine mauve (silk), and ivory.

PLATE 20

BALUCHI RUG,
Northeast Persia, Khorasan, Kashmar area,
mid 19th century.
3′8″ × 5′9″.

ONE OF THE FEW KNOWN RUGS of this field design characterised by a blue field with a central vertical row of large alternating cherry-red and violet-brown flowers flanked on either side by vertical rows of ivory flowers in diamond form. This diamond floral motif is believed to be very old (Hopf, 1962, plate 57), but it has survived through the 19th and into the 20th century in a few weavings (Black & Loveless, 1976, plates 33 & 42). The wide, cherry-red major border contains the popular 'Turkoman line' design in the colours of the field. The unusually large reciprocal 'ocean wave' secondary borders are additional features common to rugs of this area. The beauty of the lustrous wool and the blue-green lattice of the field are difficult to see except in strong light and almost impossible to photograph properly.

TECHNICAL ANALYSIS

Warp: Z2S, ivory wool, alternate warps deeply depressed.
Weft: 2Z, two shoots dark brown wool.
Pile: 2Z, wool, Persian knot open to left, 64 knots per sq. in.
Selvage: Two cables, (Z2S)4Z, wrapped in dark brown goat hair. Extensively repaired in
   dark brown wool (probably four cables originally).
Ends: Mostly missing but small amount of striped plain-weave remains.
Colours: Cherry-red, light blue, mid-blue, blue-green, violet-brown, dark brown, black,
   and ivory.

PLATE 21

BALUCHI BAG FACE, SULTAN-KHANI,
Northeast Persia, Khorasan, Kashmar area, vicinity of Kuh-e-Khab,
circa 1880.
2′0″ × 3′0″.

IT IS DIFFICULT TO IDENTIFY THIS PIECE positively as it has lost both its sides and ends. It could have been the face of a large cushion or the face of a tent bag. It may have been woven as a dowry piece as the quality of its wool, dyes and workmanship are all outstanding. The dark blue ground of the field is filled with ivory and cherry-red flowers connected by violet-brown vines which are difficult to see as they blend with the ground colour. The cherry-red major border is decorated with a dark blue and violet-brown vine meander with ivory dots at changes in direction. The reciprocal 'ocean wave' design in the dark blue and violet-brown minor borders is also difficult to see as it almost blends with the dark colours. Ivory beaded lines separate the borders.

TECHNICAL ANALYSIS
Warp: Z2S, ivory wool, level back.
Weft: 2Z, two shoots brown wool.
Pile: 2Z, wool, Persian knot open to left, 128 knots per sq. in.
Selvage: Not original.
Ends: Missing.
Colours: Cherry-red, dark blue, violet-brown, and ivory.

PLATE 22

BALUCHI RUG,
Northeast Persia, Khorasan, Nishapur area,
mid 19th century.
3′5″ × 6′3″.

THIS ATTRACTIVE OLD RUG'S blue field is covered with a lattice of thin black lines bounded in red and secured at the intersections by a small red flower with four square ivory petals arranged in a cruciform configuration. The diamond shaped lattice openings are filled with alternating rows of stylized red and coral floral rosettes. The soft coral main border is decorated with a rectangular vine medallion with hexagonal flowers in the four corners and enclosing a large central hooked rosette. This design alternates with a simple square frame enclosing a central diamond shaped flower. Split tendrils project from the vertical sides of the frame motif. This overall stylized floral design is believed to be an old Baluchi motif; it is rarely seen on rugs today.

TECHNICAL ANALYSIS
Warp: Z2S, ivory wool, level back.
Weft: 2Z, two, sometimes three, shoots brown wool.
Pile: 2Z, wool, Persian knot open to right, 80 knots per sq. in.
Selvage: Four heavy horse hair cables, wrapped in dark brown goat hair. Extensively repaired with dark brown wool.
Ends: Striped plain-weave and interlocked kilim with weft-float.
Colours: Brown-red, light coral, light blue, mid blue, dark blue, dark brown, black (corroded), and ivory.

PLATE 23

BALUCHI RUG,
Northeast Persia, Khorasan, Torbat-e-Jam region,
circa 1880.
4'10" × 7'8".

A LATTICE DESIGN OF OCTAGONS containing an 'S' figure within a rectangle at all connecting points covers the field. The honeycomb octagonal openings enclose 'Memling' güls with diamond centres each containing a cruciform flower head. The colour arrangement of the medium blue and violet-brown ground of the openings, together with the dark to light red güls, create diagonal rows. The main border contains a chain of diamonds each enclosing a cruciform flower head with a small ivory flower at the centre and at the exterior points of the petals. The main border is bounded by a stripe of ivory and violet-brown reciprocal trefoils.

TECHNICAL ANALYSIS
Warp: Z2S, ivory wool, level back.
Weft: 2Z, two shoots dark brown wool.
Pile: 2Z, wool, Persian knot open to left, 80 knots per sq. in.
Selvage: Sides overcast in dark brown wool (not original).
Ends: Plain and interlocked kilim with a central band in soumak technique and terminating in a band of small ivory weft-float flower heads.
Colours: Dark red, light red, medium blue, violet-brown (part corroded), and ivory.

PLATE 24

BALUCHI RUG,
Northeast Persia, Khorasan, Torbat-e-Jam region,
late 19th century.
3'2" × 5'11".

THE CAMEL GROUND is filled with a typical Baluchi tree-of-life with eighteen double branches each containing two quartered leaves at either side of the trunk. The light coral-red major border is decorated with an intermittent scrolling vine with split tendril flowers projecting from the top and bottom of the scrolls which are separated by diagonal ivory silk bars. The most outstanding feature is the light blue-green, star-filled, inner border which is rare in Baluchi weaving. As is customary in Baluchi work, ivory has been used most effectively to separate the borders. This fine rug may be a Timuri creation as the design and colours are a mixture of Baluchi and Timuri work.

TECHNICAL ANALYSIS
Warp: Z2S, ivory wool, level back.
Weft: 2Z, two shoots brown wool.
Pile: 2Z, wool and silk, Persian knot open to left, 112 knots per sq. in.
Selvage: Four cables, (Z2S)3Z, wrapped in dark brown goat hair.
Ends: Top – two inch band of striped plain-weave kilim (reduced); bottom – missing.
Colours: Light coral-red, camel, violet-brown, blue-green, dark blue, ivory wool and silk.

PLATE 25

BALUCHI RU-KORSSI,
Northeast Persia, Khorasan region,
circa 1870.
3'2" × 3'5".

THE VARIEGATED LIGHT RED FIELD of this beautifully crafted little table-cover is decorated with a small saffron cock in each corner. To the nomad, the cock was a herald of glory and victory which drove away the night and protected the home from evil. A row of precisely drawn black forms in weft-float with a squarish base and split tendrils projecting from the sides frames the field. The border contains a continuous row of alternating ivory snowflakes and red and blue floral forms in soumak technique. The ends of the piece are elaborately decorated in weft-float. A rare piece once proudly displayed in some Baluchi weaver's tent.

TECHNICAL ANALYSIS
Warp: Z2S, ivory wool, 16 warps per linear inch.
Weft: 2Z, wool, 22 field design wefts per linear inch.
Selvage: Four cables, Z3S, ivory wool wrapped in brown goat hair.
Ends: Plain-weave with four bands of weft-float separated by three bands of chain-stitch;
   kilim turned over and sewn down at the ends.
Colours: Light red, saffron, light blue, dark blue, black, and ivory.

PLATE 26

BALUCHI RU-KORSSI,
Northeast Persia, Khorasan region,
circa 1875.
3′10″ × 3′11″.

THE PLAIN-WOVEN LIGHT RED FIELD is decorated with a central floral diamond form constructed from very closely spaced concentric lines of multicoloured soumak brocade with axial stems emerging from the diamond points and ending in a smaller diamond flower. Black plain-weave interlocking serrated triangles project from the border into the field. As is common in Baluchi ru-korssi design, these forms are larger at the sides than at the ends. The black border contains a central row of small floral rosettes in weft-float. The piece has been carefully preserved with a number of reweaves in the red field indicating that it was highly valued by its former owner.

TECHNICAL ANALYSIS
Warp: Z2S, ivory wool, 16 warps per linear inch.
Weft: Z2, wool, 20 field design wefts per linear inch.
Selvage: Six cables of Z4S ivory wool wrapped in brown wool and decorated with three rows of multicoloured slanted flat-stitch in a herringbone pattern.
Ends: Plain-weave with three rows of red, gold and blue chain-stitch; kilim turned over and sewn down at the ends.
Colours: Soft light red, light blue, cobalt-blue, dark blue, gold, brown, green, mole-grey, black, and ivory.

PLATE 27

BALUCHI RU-KORSSI,
Northeast Persia, Khorasan region,
late 19th century.
4'5" × 4'6".

A RARE AND BEAUTIFUL SQUARE WEAVING composed almost
entirely of borders in various flat-weave techniques and a small, striking
central panel of natural camel hair decorated with a stepped gül with floral
stem projections in polychrome weft-wrapping and the usual border of
black hooked triangles – unusual here in that they are approximately the
same size at the ends and sides of the field. Equally rare are the dark brown
goat hair stripes bounding the guards to the inner border. The piece is
woven in the sombre dark colours so beloved by the Baluchi, but its
appearance is enlivened by the ivory motifs used to highlight the design.
This is probably a *sofreh-ye'aqd*, or wedding sofreh, which a bride would
use as a ru-korssi in her new home. The central panel once contained an
inscription and a date which have been almost entirely worn away.

TECHNICAL ANALYSIS
Warp: Z2S, light brown and ivory wool, 14 warps per linear inch.
Weft: Z2, natural camel hair (central panel), 18 ground wefts per linear inch.
Selvage: Eight cables, Z4S, brown and ivory wool, wrapped in four cords. The inner and outer
    cords in dark brown goat hair and the centre cords in coloured wool.
Ends: Plain-weave kilim with two bands of double running-stitch and two bands of weft-float.
    The kilim is turned over and sewn down at both ends.
Colours: Natural camel, light red, brown-red, gold, light blue, dark blue, dark brown, green,
    black, and ivory.

PLATE 28

BALUCHI RU-KORSSI,
Northeast Persia, Khorasan region,
circa 1900.
4′0″ × 4′2″.

THIS RUG PRESENTS AN ENIGMA as the workmanship is of the finest quality, indicating a 19th century creation, but some of the dyes used in the cotton floral rosettes of the end panels appear mostly in weavings of the 20th century. There is little doubt, however, that it is the work of a highly skilled weaver, probably in a sedentary or semi-sedentary environment. It is not unique since at least two others (Black and Loveless, 1976, plate 9 and Herrmann, 1984, plate 77) have surfaced in the last twelve years; but it is, nevertheless, a rare example in excellent condition. All three have the same colouring and general design, but this piece is slightly smaller, having a narrower main border.

TECHNICAL ANALYSIS
Warp: Z2S, ivory wool, alternate warps deeply depressed.
Weft: 2Z, two, sometimes three, shoots brown wool.
Pile: 2Z, wool, Persian knot open to right, 100 knots per sq. in.
Selvage: Four cables, Z8S, wrapped with dark brown goat hair.
Ends: Plain-weave kilim with weft-float and soumak brocade. Stylized flowers (small serrated diamond forms) contain yellow cotton thread wrapped with metal and multicoloured mercerised cotton.
Colours: Light red, dark blue, purple-brown, black, ivory, terracotta, mauve, yellow-green, purple, and brown-gold metal thread.

PLATE 29

BALUCHI SALT BAG,
Northeast Persia, Khorasan region,
circa 1900.
1′5″x 1′6″.

PILE-WOVEN SALT BAGS of this type are rare and there is little agreement on their source. In this particularly fine example the top and bottom flat-woven end bands and several of the field designs are highlighted with multicoloured mercerised cotton. This, in addition to the fine weave, colours and other characteristics, indicate that it was probably woven in the same area as the preceding ru-korssi. Also, like the ru-korssi, the true beauty of its design cannot be revealed in a photograph due to its dark colours.

TECHNICAL ANALYSIS

Warp: Z2S, ivory wool, alternate warps deeply depressed.

Weft: 2Z, two shoots brown wool.

Pile: Wool and mercerised cotton, Persian knot open to left, 160 knots per sq. in.

Selvage: Four cables, Z3S, ivory wool, wrapped in black goat hair. Sides closed with a raised fishbone-stitch in black goat hair.

Ends: Face – top and bottom end bands in multicoloured mercerised cotton soumak brocade; back – black plain-weave kilim with top and bottom end bands in weft-float.

Colours: Brown-red, dark violet-brown, dark blue, black and ivory with mercerised cotton in purple-red, light blue, gold, and beige.

PLATE 30

BALUCHI SOFREH,
Northeast Persia, Khorasan region,
circa 1870.
2′4″ × 4′6″.

A CHARMING SMALL SOFREH with a plain-woven camel field decorated with an unusual tree containing multicoloured leafy branches resembling rays of light. The sides of the field are decorated with typical interlocking brown triangles which become delicate reciprocal trefoils at the ends of the field. The broad ends (or skirts) are elaborately adorned with designs in several flat-woven techniques, including the popular weft-float and soumak types. The field is enclosed by four borders. Two of these – the boxed diamond and reciprocal 'ocean wave' – are highlighted in bleached ivory. A rare piece with unusually fresh colours considering its apparent age.

TECHNICAL ANALYSIS
Warp: Z2S, ivory wool, 18 warps per linear inch.
Weft: 2Z, wool, 20 ground wefts per linear inch.
Selvage: Not original.
Ends: Four principal bands – two in soumak, one weft-float and one plain-woven – all separated by lines of chain-stitch. A partial fifth band of ivory plain-weave decorated with a chain of diamonds with tendrils projecting from the vertical points, is shown almost complete at the top end.
Colours: Camel, coral-red, turquoise, mid blue, dark brown, surmey (blue-black), gold, and ivory.

PLATE 31

BALUCHI SOFREH,
Northeast Persia, Khorasan region,
circa 1875.
2'7" × 5'2".

FLAT-WOVEN RUGS of this type are occasionally found, especially in Baluchi weaving, but seldom do we encounter one of this quality. The design reminds one of a window with upper and lower plain-woven camel hair 'glass' panes through which a forest or garden can be seen with animals and other forms appearing among the trees – all rendered in soumak or other weft-wrapping techniques. These visions are contained in a flat-woven frame composed of a major border decorated with a continuous repeat of an elongated hexagon alternating with a diamond form and separated by opposing half diamonds in ivory. Reciprocal 'ocean wave' secondary borders are rendered in brown-red and ivory. The piece is highlighted throughout in silk.

TECHNICAL ANALYSIS

Warp: Z2S, ivory wool, 16 warps per linear inch.
Weft: Z2, natural camel hair, 20 ground wefts per linear inch.
Selvage: Two cables, Z2S, wrapped in dark brown goat hair.
Ends: Six inch plain-woven striped and interlocked kilim with two inch band of weft-float.
Colours: Coral-red, brown-red, camel hair, dark brown, light blue, dark blue, magenta (silk),
   gold (silk), and ivory.

PLATE 32

BALUCHI PILLOW (BALISHT),
Northeast Persia, Khorasan region,
mid 19th century.
1′7″ × 2′5″.

WHEN A. CECIL EDWARDS STATED "Camel hair is also used in the
finest quality Balishts – some of the finest examples of Baluchi weaving are
to be found among them", he could have been describing this charming
little pillow, which surely is a treasure of the type that every Baluchi rug
collector looks for. The pile is closely clipped and all design elements, from
the delicately drawn reciprocal trefoils guarding the inner border, to the
dainty little tree-of-life with silken highlights, are of exceptional merit.
The piece is complete except for the missing closure stitch at the sides.

TECHNICAL ANALYSIS
Warp: Z2S, ivory wool, alternate warps deeply depressed.
Weft: 2Z, two shoots brown wool.
Pile: 2Z, wool and camel hair. Persian knot open to left, 192 knots per sq. in.
Selvage: Two cables, 6Z, wrapped in brown wool.
Ends: One and a half inch plain-weave with weft-float band bounded by a line of red and blue
   outline stitch.
Colours: Camel, dark brown, deep brown-red, apricot, black (corroded), green-gold (silk),
   and ivory.

PLATE 33

BALUCHI BAG FACE,
Northeast Persia, Khorasan region,
third quarter 19th century.
2′6″ × 2′11″.

THE DARK BLUE FIELD of this piece contains a central dark brown squarish panel with a reciprocal trefoil frame in purple-red and dark blue. This panel is centred on a large eight-pointed star within an ivory octagon and surrounded by plant and geometric forms, including the dark blue stylized bird or animal in the four corners of the panel facing the star. The field surrounding the square is filled with eighteen smaller stars-in-octagons. The main ivory border is decorated with a vine meander with red floral pennants. The secondary borders are composed of reciprocal trefoil forms in coral-red and dark blue. One of the oldest and most common Baluchi cushion and bag designs, here woven in soft, lustrous wool.

TECHNICAL ANALYSIS
Warp: Z2S, ivory wool, alternate warps slightly depressed.
Weft: 2Z, two shoots dark brown wool.
Pile: 2Z, wool, Persian knot open to left, 90 knots per sq. in.
Selvage: Two cables, Z3S & Z4S, ivory wool wrapped in brown wool.
Ends: Top – plain-weave with weft-float; bottom – missing.
Colours: Coral-red, purple-red, mid-blue, dark blue, dark brown, apricot, and ivory.

PLATE 34

BALUCHI BAG FACE,
Northeast Persia, Khorasan region,
third quarter 19th century.
2'6" × 2'9".

HERE THE WEAVER HAS OMITTED the border to the violet-brown panel typically centred on an ivory star-in-octogon, allowing the small coral-red flowers of the field to merge with the stylized plants and animal forms of the panel. The panel is framed by the usual star-in-octogon forms, but the weaver has added interest by alternating the white stars with a smaller star-in-blue octagon at the top and bottom of the field, while an attractive coral-red floral rosette has been added to the sides. The usual vine meander with red floral pennants decorates the major border, which is guarded by brown and red barber pole stripes.

TECHNICAL ANALYSIS

Warp: Z2S, ivory wool, alternate warps moderately depressed.
Weft: 2Z, two shoots dark brown wool.
Pile: 2Z, wool, Persian knot open to left, 110 knots per sq. in.
Selvage: Two cables, ivory wool wrapped in brown wool.
Ends: Top – plain-weave with weft-float band of 'S' figures with chain-stitch guards;
    bottom – missing.
Colours: Coral-red, brown-red, mid-blue, dark blue, violet-brown, light brown, and ivory.

PLATE 35

BALUCHI BAG FACE,
Northeast Persia, Khorasan region,
circa 1870.
2'6" × 2'7".

SIMILAR TO THE TWO PRECEDING EXAMPLES, with the same general design of a dark blue field and violet-brown central panel with a large star-in-octagon and surrounded by smaller stars-in-octagons. In this case the principal differences are the striking light electric-blue used in the trees projecting from the top and bottom central star-in-octagon and the borders of alternate surrounding octagons. Magenta silk has been added to the trunk decoration of the top tree. The use of the special light blue colour, the magenta silk and the fine, soft, lustrous wool in which the piece was woven all indicate that no effort was spared in making this treasured personal possession.

TECHNICAL ANALYSIS

Warp: Z2S, ivory wool, smooth back.
Weft: 2Z, two shoots dark brown wool.
Pile: 2Z, wool and silk, Persian knot open to left, 108 knots per sq. in.
Selvage: Not original.
Ends: Missing.
Colours: Brick-red, light coral-red, light blue, dark blue, magenta (silk), violet-brown
    (corroded), and ivory.

PLATE 36

BALUCHI PILLOW (POSHTI),
Northeast Persia, Khorasan region,
circa 1880.
2'0" × 2'2".

SQUARE PIECES SUCH AS THIS, without closure loops or slits, were used as back pillows (Wegner, 1980, Table 1). They were filled with cotton and the top and open sides were sewn up. In this case the field is covered by a thin blue lattice with small diamond flower heads at the connecting points. The lattice has octagonal openings containing red or ivory eight-pointed stars in diagonal rows. The rust-red major border contains 'S' repeats resembling pairs of opposing cocks – the Baluchi symbol of authority and leadership. Firdawsi reported them as wearing such crests in early times. The outer border contains a row of ivory pentagonal lappet forms with points projecting inward, while the inner border contains the more familiar reciprocal trefoil forms bounded by ivory beaded lines.

TECHNICAL ANALYSIS
Warp: Z2S, ivory wool, slight depression of alternate warps.
Weft: 2Z, two shoots dark brown wool.
Pile:; 2Z, wool, Persian knot open to the left, 108 knots per sq. in.
Selvage: Sides closed with a raised fish-bone stitch in dark brown goat hair.
Ends: Top – one inch plain-weave kilim with a quarter inch line of ivory weft-float. Top
   (open) ends of front and back are bound by the raised fish-bone stitch in blue wool.
Colours: Rust-red, violet-brown, dark olive-brown (slightly corroded), medium blue,
   and ivory.

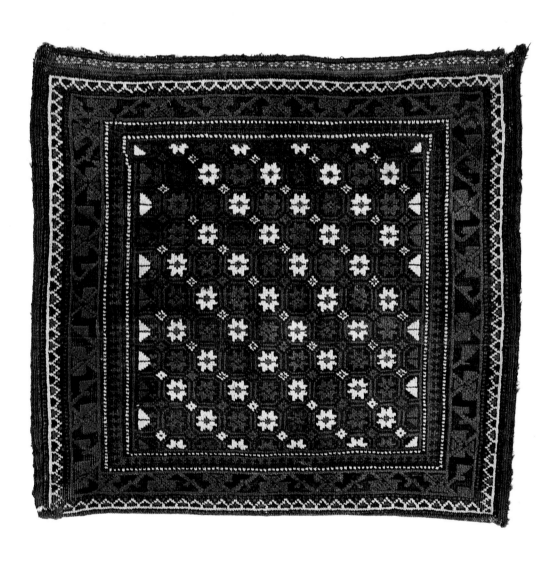

PLATE 37

BALUCHI PILLOW FACE,
Northeast Persia, Khorasan region,
circa 1880.
1'10" × 2'11".

THE FIELD OF THIS PIECE contains six hexagons arranged in two vertical rows. The hexagons are highlighted by a group of three ivory triangles with points projecting outward from the top and bottom of the hexagons. The remainder of the medium blue field is filled with red plant and geometric forms. The central plant form is woven in olive-green and outlined in red. The brown-red outer border contains a blue vine and leaf 'S' scroll resembling the common 'wave' pattern. The centre border contains another 'S' form and is guarded by small ivory, red, and blue flowerheads in a five-spot motif. A chain of reciprocal red and blue split tendril, or ram's horn, motifs constitutes the inner border. It is assumed that this was originally the face of a pillow as it shows no evidence of having had closure slits and loops as would be required for a bag.

TECHNICAL ANALYSIS

Warp: Z2S, ivory wool, alternate warps slightly depressed.
Weft: 2Z, two shoots dark brown wool.
Pile: 2Z, Persian knot open to left, 99 knots per sq. in.
Selvage: One cable, (Z2S)4Z, overcast in dark brown wool.
Ends: Top – one inch plain-weave kilim with a quarter inch band of ivory weft-float bounded by double rows of weft twining; bottom – two inch plain-weave kilim with one inch band of red and ivory weft-float.
Colours: Light red, brown-red, medium blue, dark brown (corroded), olive-green, and ivory.

PLATE 38

BALUCHI PRAYER RUG,
Northeast Persia, Khorasan, Sarakhs area,
circa 1875.
2'5" × 4'1".

ANOTHER LOVELY PRAYER RUG with the field of the mihrab piled in a warm shade of natural camel hair which is impossible to equal with dyes. The stylized tree-of-life has a slightly different arrangement of branches and leaves. The spandrels are woven in a like manner with camel hair, but the central plant form is much simpler. The entire mihrab is delicately drawn without overcrowding. The five typical borders framing the mihrab are skilfully executed and the colours harmoniously blended.

TECHNICAL ANALYSIS
Warp: Z2S, ivory wool, smooth back.
Weft: 2Z, two shoots brown wool.
Pile: 2Z, wool and camel hair, Persian knot open to left, 120 knots per sq. in.
Selvage: Two cables, Z4S, wrapped in dark brown wool.
Colours: Copper-red, brown-red, ruby-red (cochineal), natural camel, light blue, dark blue, black (corroded), and ivory (bleached).
Literature: See *Turkoman Rugs* by Amos Bateman Thacher, New York 1940, plate 51.

PLATE 39

BALUCHI PRAYER RUG,
Northeast Persia, Khorasan, Sarakhs area,
late 19th century.
2'4" × 3'4".

THE CAMEL FIELD contains a typical tree-of-life with leafy branches and a hooked diamond medallion at the top and bottom. The top medallion is enclosed by a barber pole ribbon in dark blue and red. All empty spaces are filled with eight-pointed stars, 'S' figures and tiny cruciform devices. The primary border at either side contains a chain of stylized flower heads with a blue cruciform centre. The outer border has a red and white lappet form with its points projecting outward. The piece contains several unusual design features; for example the small camel panels at either side of the niche at the top contain three anchor forms reminiscent of those in the Yomut *Kepse*-gül; the slender central border with the familiar Turkoman 'tuning fork' devices; and the wedge-shaped bottom of the niche with the resulting triangular corners of the field.

TECHNICAL ANALYSIS
Warp: Z2S, ivory wool, alternate warps slightly depressed.
Weft: 2Z, two shoots brown wool.
Pile: 2Z, wool, Persian knot opens to left, 117 knots per sq. in.
Selvage: Two cables, (Z2S)3Z, wrapped in dark brown goat hair.
Ends: Five inch plain-weave kilim with two and a half inch interlocked deep-toothed panel bounded by a quarter inch weft-float ivory stripe and terminating in a one inch band in soumak technique.
Colours: Coral-red, brown-red, camel, light brown, dark brown, medium blue, and ivory.

PLATE 40

BALUCHI BAG, RAHIM-KHANI,
Northeast Persia, Khorasan, Sarakhs area,
circa 1880.
2'8" × 2'10".

THE DOMINANT FEATURE of this piece is the pair of large Salor-type güls which adorn the face of the bag. Two central stepped, hooked half diamond forms project from the sides of the field with quarter forms appearing at the corners. Two small goats at the right and left of the güls complete the picture. The terracotta major border is decorated with dark blue lobed flower heads highlighted with four small ivory crosses. These flower heads alternate with stylized vine and leaf forms. Secondary borders contain the popular reciprocal 'ocean wave' design in brown-red and dark blue. The inner border is filled with a chain of alternating terracotta and brown-red snowflakes with ivory highlights. The borders are separated by thin beaded ivory lines. The piece is finely woven in specially selected, lustrous wool.

TECHNICAL ANALYSIS
Warp: Z2S, ivory wool, smooth back.
Weft: 2Z, two shoots dark brown wool.
Pile: 2Z, wool, Persian knot open to left, 126 knots per sq. in.
Selvage: Two cables, Z6S, ivory wool wrapped in dark brown wool. Closure stitch is missing.
Ends: Top – plain-weave with one and half inch band of weft-float having chain-stitch guards.
    End folded and sewn down; bottom – plain-weave decorated with a line of raised fish-bone stitch in dark brown goat hair.
Colours: Brown-red, terracotta, dark blue, black (corroded), and ivory.
Literature: See *Rugs of the Wandering Baluchi* by David Black and Clive Loveless, London 1976,
    p. 17, plate 1, for a very similar piece.

PLATE 41

BALUCHI RUG,
Northeast Persia, Khorasan, Sarakhs area,
third quarter 19th century.
1'8" × 3'8".

A LARGE QUARTERED GÜL has been placed in the centre of the dark
blue field of this attractive small rug. Two quarters of this gül are in coral-
red and the other two are in dark blue. The gül encloses a flattened
hexagon with a mahogany perimeter and a dark blue centre which contains
a rosette with four ivory and four mahogany petals. This large gül has been
extended along the vertical axis with purple-red panels above and below,
each decorated with floral rosettes and other flower and plant forms. The
remaining open spaces in the blue field have been filled with eight-pointed
stars and stylized plant and floral forms. The mahogany major border
contains a chain of outward pointing diamond centred spear-heads. The
dark blue outer border is decorated with a reciprocal trefoil motif outlined
in red, and the borders are bounded by thin lines of beaded ivory stripes. It
is woven in carefully selected, high quality wool which is soft and velvet-
like to the touch and reflects light in an attractive, lustrous sheen. The rug
may have been woven as a large cushion or pillow face, but apparently was
never used as such. It has been assigned to the Sarakhs area due to the
extensive use of Turkoman motifs, particularly the anchor design of the
Yomut *Kepse*-gül in the chain of small squares bounding the field.

TECHNICAL ANALYSIS
Warp: Z2S, ivory wool, level back.
Weft: 2Z, two shoots dark brown wool.
Pile: 2Z, wool, Persian knot open to left, 108 knots per sq. in.
Selvage: Two cables, (Z2S)4Z, wrapped in dark brown wool.
Ends: Plain-weave decorated with weft-float chain of 'S' figures.
Colours: Coral-red, purple-red, mahogany-red, dark blue, medium blue, dark brown, black
   (corroded), and ivory.
Published: Baluchi Rugs by Jeff Boucher and H. McCoy Jones, Washington D.C.
   1974, no. 15.

PLATE 42

BALUCHI PILLOW OR STORAGE BAG,
Northeast Persia, southern Khorasan,
early 20th century.
1'10" × 3'6".

PILLOWS (BAGS) OF THIS TYPE were woven by members of many Baluchi and non-Baluchi tribal units in northeastern Persia and northwestern Afghanistan. This example displays the characteristic sombre Baluchi colouring, highlighted by accents of ivory in the secondary borders and flat-woven ends. A rust-red major border decorated with stylized flowering vines and beaded tassels along one side adds additional interest to the piece.

TECHNICAL ANALYSIS
Warp: Z2S, ivory wool, level back.
Weft: 2Z, two shoots brown wool.
Pile: 2Z, wool, Persian knot, open to left, 63 knots per sq. in.
Selvage: Sides closed with a raised fish-bone stitch in dark brown goat hair.
Ends: Top – plain and slit weave kilim with weft-float and stem-stitch guards. Dark brown
   goat hair closure loops; bottom – plain-weave with weft-float and stem-stitch guards.
Colours: Dark rust-red, violet-brown, apricot, medium blue, dark brown, black, and ivory.
Published: The Oriental Rug Collection of Jerome and Mary Jane Straka, New York 1978, no. 49.

PLATE 43

BALUCHI PILLOW OR STORAGE BAG,
Northeast Persia, southern Khorasan,
early 20th century.
1'8" × 3'3".

THE BOTEH IS A FAVOURITE DESIGN in many weaving areas of Persia, and Khorasan is no exception. Here a Baluchi weaver has covered the dark blue field of this piece with small botehs, in predominately rust-red and red-brown colours, at the top of a leafy stem in the manner of a flower. The main border is decorated with a stylized vine and leaf motif resembling a chain of 'S' forms. The red and blue striped guard borders are highlighted by ivory dots separating the colours. A close look is required to distinguish the reciprocal 'ocean wave' design in the outer border. In fact the entire pillow face appears a sombre brownish-blue and the design forms are only clearly revealed by strong light. The overall dark colours are most difficult to photograph properly. The back has alternating bands of weft-float and interlocked plain-weave in a chevron design, guarded by double rows of weft twining.

TECHNICAL ANALYSIS
Warp: Z2S, ivory wool, moderate alternate warp depression.
Weft: 2Z, two shoots dark brown wool.
Pile: 2Z, wool, Persian knot open to left, 130 knots per sq. in.
Selvage: Sides closed with a raised fish-bone stitch in dark brown goat hair.
Ends: Top – plain-weave with two ivory weft-float bands separated by a red and brown chain-stitch line guarded by double rows of weft twining, red and brown wool closure loops; bottom – narrow ivory band in weft-float technique.
Colours: Rust-red, red-brown, violet-brown, dark brown, apricot, medium blue, dark blue, dark olive-green, and ivory.

PLATE 44

BALUCHI PRAYER RUG, BAHLURI,
Northeast Persia, Khorasan, Qainat area,
circa 1870.
2′6″ × 4′9″.

THERE IS LITTLE AGREEMENT in the West regarding the symbolism expressed in prayer rugs of the Middle East, and those of the Baluchi are no exception. However, one cannot escape the religious contemplation that inspired the weaver who created this small masterpiece. One could believe that she became so absorbed in her work that she moved in a mystical trance as she raised herself above the harsh reality of the world in which she lived. For example, she probably perceived the mihrab with its three flowering trees-of-life as the 'gateway to paradise', and the dark blue ground beyond as eternity (Cammann, 1972, p. 19). Three borders frame this heavenly view. Half of the inner border is rendered in brilliant coral-red which serves as a beacon for this view of paradise. In the brown-red spandrels above the mihrab shoulders the weaver has placed two large dark blue hands with long slender extended fingers – an ancient Islamic symbol of protection for one engaged in prayer. A carefully made rug which could easily be dated to the middle of the 19th century except for the mauve dye which alternates with light blue in the barber pole main body of the trees. This tip-faded purple is believed to be one of the first synthetic aniline dyes to reach the Baluchi weaving area of Khorasan. A rare rug finely woven in the best silky wool.

TECHNICAL ANALYSIS
Warp; Z2S, ivory wool, level back.
Weft: 2Z, two, sometimes three, shoots brown wool.
Pile: 2Z, wool, Turkish knot points to lower left, 154 knots per sq. in.
Selvage: Two cords of two ivory wool cables, (Z2S)3Z, wrapped in dark brown goat hair
    (repaired in dark brown wool).
Ends: Four inches of weft-float technique in five bands.
Colours: Coral-red, brown-red, dark brown, dark blue, light blue, light green, tip-faded
    mauve, and ivory.
Literature: See *Ballard Collection of Oriental Rugs in the City Art Museum of St. Louis* by Maurice
    S. Dimand, St. Louis 1935, plate LXV.

PLATE 45

BALUCHI RUG, BAHLURI,
Northeast Persia, Khorasan, Qainat area,
late 19th century.
2'11" × 5'3".

AN ATTRACTIVE RUG with soft, velvety pile. The primary field design of octagon güls enclosing four elongated hexagons with 'S' forms is believed to be very old. This design is rarely used on rugs, but is occasionally found on old bag faces. The major border contains a repeating box-flower design while the minor borders appear as ivory pentagonal lappet forms and in a saw-toothed form at the sides. A pleasing variation is found in the unusual violet-brown pile-woven end panels with a central band of camel hair containing a red and blue vine meander and framed by a medium blue stripe.

TECHNICAL ANALYSIS
Warp: Z2S, ivory wool, alternate warps slightly depressed.
Weft: 2Z, two shoots brown wool.
Pile: 2Z, wool and camel hair (end panels), Turkish knot points to the right, 108 knots per sq. in.
Selvage: Four cables, ivory wool, (Z2S)4Z, wrapped in dark brown goat hair.
Ends: One and a half inch plain striped kilim.
Colours: Brick-red, light blue, medium blue, violet-brown, dark brown (corroded), natural camel and ivory.

PLATE 46

BALUCHI RUG,
Northeast Persia, Khorasan, Qainat area,
third quarter 19th century.
3'1" × 5'9".

THIS IS A RARE TYPE of Baluchi weaving distinguished by rows of
Turkoman-like güls filled with eight-pointed stars and set on an unusually
clear light red field. Small tree forms, combs, stars and stylized flowers fill
the voids between the güls. The ivory major border filled with box-flowers
in the colours of the field is unusual in rugs with this Turkoman design,
while the design in the inside secondary border of closely linked diamond
forms with a black cruciform central motif is rarely found in these rugs.
The elaborate kilim aprons are common in fine rugs of this type.

TECHNICAL ANALYSIS
Warp: Z2S, ivory wool, level back.
Weft: 2Z, two shoots brown wool.
Pile: 2Z, wool, Persian knot open to left, 96 knots per sq. in.
Selvage: Four cables, Z7S, wrapped in dark brown goat hair.
Ends: Plain-weave and interlocked kilim with one band of weft-float.
Colours: Clear light red, clear light blue, dark blue, dark brown (corroded), black (corroded),
    and ivory.
Literature: See *HALI*, Vol. 3, no. 1, 1980, p. 33, fig. 3.

PLATE 47

BALUCHI RUG,
Northeast Persia, Khorasan, Qainat area,
late 19th century.
3′1″ × 5′8″.

THIS ATTRACTIVE RUG has a corroded olive-brown field with diagonal rows of hooked Memling güls in cherry-red and maroon, with a major border in colours of the field highlighted by a stylized ivory rosette in the middle of each side and ivory highlighted guard borders. The red güls stand out from the corroded brown field and major border in an imposing, sculpted manner. The piece has obviously been preserved in a collection without use for many years as indicated by the fine condition of its selvages and kilim ends.

TECHNICAL ANALYSIS
Warp: Z2S, ivory wool, alternate warps moderately depressed.
Weft: 2Z, two shoots brown wool.
Pile: 2Z, wool, Persian knot open to left, 80 knots per sq. in.
Selvage: Two cables (Z9S) overcast as one cord with dark brown goat hair.
Ends: Five inch striped plain and interlocked kilim with running stitch guards.
Colours: Cherry-red, maroon, olive-brown (corroded), dark brown, and ivory (bleached).
Provenance: Formerly in the Aram K. Jerrehian Collection, Philadelphia, Pennsylvania.

PLATE 48

BALUCHI BAG FACE,
Northeast Persia, Khorasan, Qainat area,
circa 1870.
2′4″ × 2′8″.

THIS IS THE FACE of half of a large double saddle bag. The dark blue field is covered by five horizontal rows of stylized peacocks in red and brown with the central one in ivory, red and brown. Note the void at the right which is filled by stylized trees and two birds in half form. The ivory main border is decorated with repeating floral stems bearing pairs of opposed red and brown leaves and diamond flowers in full bloom. The plain-woven band at the top with slits originally retained the horse hair loops used for closure.

TECHNICAL ANALYSIS
Warp: Z2S, ivory wool, alternate warps slightly depressed.
Weft: 2Z, two shoots dark brown wool.
Pile: 2Z, wool, Persian knot open to left, 88 knots per sq. in.
Selvage: Two cables, Z4S, wrapped in dark brown wool.
Ends: Top – plain slit-tapestry with two bands of weft-float; bottom – plain-weave kilim.
Colours: Dark purple-red, light red, light brown, dark brown, dark blue, and ivory.
Literature: See *Ballard Collection of Oriental Rugs* by J.A. MacLean and D. Blair, St. Louis
    1924, no. 103.

PLATE 49

BALUCHI PILLOW OR STORAGE BAG,
Southeast Persia, Sistan area,
early 20th century.
1′8″ × 3′4″.

PILE BAGS OF THIS TYPE are rare in the Sistan-Baluchistan area where most such items are flat-woven. The overall brownish colour of this piece, together with its decorations, indicate an origin somewhere in Sistan, which may extend eastward to Chakhansur in Afghanistan. The central camel-coloured field is framed by a reciprocal trefoil motif and contains a characteristic tree-of-life with Turkoman 'tuning fork' designs decorating the trunk. The floral border is bounded by beaded ivory guard stripes and one side is embellished with a row of crude glass beads and woollen tassels.

TECHNICAL ANALYSIS

Warp : Z2S, natural ivory wool mixed with some natural brown wool, level back.
Weft: 2Z, two shoots brown wool.
Pile: 2Z, wool, Persian knot open to left, 84 knots per sq. in.
Selvage: Sides closed with a raised fish-bone stitch in dark brown goat hair.
Ends: Plain-weave with weft-float decoration and stem-stitch guards.
Colours: Dark pinkish-red, violet-brown, dark brown, orange, black and ivory.
Published: Baluchi Rugs by Jeff Boucher and H. McCoy Jones, Washington, D.C. 1974,
    plate 45.

PLATE 50

BALUCHI VANITY BAG,
Southeast Persia, Sistan, Zabol area,
early 20th century.
1′2″ × 1′2″.

THIS SMALL DOUBLE-SIDED BAG is made from a single piled panel
which has been folded and joined down the sides. Each pile face is almost
identical in design. Principal features are the central cruciform device in
magenta silk and the seven elaborate side tassels decorated with shells.

TECHNICAL ANALYSIS
Warp: Z2S, ivory wool, level back.
Weft: 2Z, two shoots brown wool.
Pile: 2Z, wool and silk, Persian knot open to left, 154 knots per sq. in.
Selvage: Sides closed in a raised fish-bone stitch in dark brown goat hair.
Ends: Top – one inch kilim decorated with a band of seven rows of chain-stitch in red, black
    and ivory. The warp ends are turned under and sewn down.
Colours: Light red, brown-red, dark brown, dark blue, green, black, magenta (silk), and
    ivory.
Literature: For a flat-woven example see *Textiles of Baluchistan* by M.G. Konieczny, London
    1979, plate 34.

PLATE 51

BALUCHI RUG,
Baluchistan region, Pakistan-Afghanistan border area,
circa 1920.
3′10″ × 7′10″.

A STRIKING ALL WOOL FLAT-WOVEN RUG with a horizontal striped violet-brown kilim central field containing three principal brown-red horizontal panels, each decorated with three multicoloured, interlocked, stepped medallions separated by bands of weft-float. A magnificent frame of seven weft-float ivory borders encloses the central field. According to M.G. Konieczny, pieces of this size are called floor rugs while larger sizes are referred to as bedding covers. They are woven by Baluchi tribes on both sides of the Pakistan-Afghanistan border.

TECHNICAL ANALYSIS
Warp: Z2S, ivory wool, 12 warps per linear inch.
Weft: 2Z, wool, 18 ground wefts per linear inch.
Selvage: Six cables, (Z2S)3Z, wrapped in multicoloured wool, first and sixth cable additionally wrapped in dark brown goat hair which has mostly worn away from the outer cable.
Ends: Striped plain-weave kilim. Warp ends knotted in groups of three and four.
Colours: Brown-red, violet-brown, dark brown, light blue, medium blue-green, orange, pale pink and ivory.
Published: Baluchi Rugs by Jeff Boucher and H. McCoy Jones, Washington D.C. 1974, no. 30.
Literature: See *Textiles of Baluchistan* by M.G. Konieczny, London 1979, plate 1.

THE PLATES
PART II

BALUCHI IN NAME ONLY
PLATES 52-65

A select few from the many woven items sold in
the trade as Baluchi but actually woven by other
neighbouring ethnic groups.

PLATE 52

KURD BALUCHI RUG,
Northeast Persia, Khorasan, Nishapur-Sabzevar area,
late 19th century.
2'10" × 5'3".

THE PRECISELY DRAWN RED DIAMOND LATTICE of the field
encloses blue and brown-violet hooked diamond forms with a cruciform
centre. The brown-violet major border is decorated with blue and red
rectangles containing hooked forms. The camel hair secondary borders
contain unusual depressed reciprocal 'ocean wave' forms separated by
diagonal blue and brown bars dotted in red. Rugs of this type are usually
attributed to Kurdish weavers living in the area between Nishapur and
Sabzevar.

TECHNICAL ANALYSIS
Warp: Z2S, ivory (some brown) wool, alternate warps slightly depressed.
Weft: 2Z, two shoots ivory or brown wool.
Pile: 2Z, wool and camel hair, Turkish knot points to right, 98 knots per sq. in.
Selvage: Two cords of three warps each wrapped in light brown wool or dark brown goat hair.
Ends: Two inch plain ivory kilim decorated with 'X' forms in the colours of the field.
Colours: Light blue, mid blue, coral-red, light brown, dark brown, brown-violet, camel hair,
    black (corroded), and white.

PLATE 53

TIMURI RUG, YAQUB-KHANI,
Northeast Persia, Khorasan, Torbat-e-Jam, Zurabad area,
late 19th century.
2'8" × 4'9".

THE FIELD OF THIS SMALL RUG is decorated with a lattice
containing rectangular openings each filled by a diamond rosette with split
tendrils projecting from the points. This motif is generally used in the field
of Yaqub-Khani prayer rugs, but it is occasionally found in other rugs as
well. An outstanding rug which many would overlook due to its sombre
reddish-blue colour. The unusually glossy sheen and soft, silky texture are
due to the specially selected wool from which it was woven, plus a possible
admixture of goat-fleece. The fine, predominantly blue and red wool
reflects a violet sheen, or bloom, in strong light. Because of its lustre and
dark colours, no photograph can do true justice to this rug.

TECHNICAL ANALYSIS
Warp: Z2S, ivory wool, level back.
Weft: 2Z, two shoots dark brown and black wool.
Pile: 2Z, wool, Persian knot open to left, 88 knots per sq. in.
Selvage: Four cables, 6Z-9Z, wrapped in dark brown goat hair.
Ends: Striped plain-weave kilim with two inch band in soumak technique.
Colours: Light coral-red, dark wine-red, light brown, dark brown, light blue, dark blue,
   black, gold, and ivory.

PLATE 54

TIMURI CARPET, YAQUB-KHANI,
Northwest Afghanistan, Herat province, Gulran district,
mid 19th century.
5'4" × 7'8".

WOVEN IN THE FINEST SILKY WOOL, this is probably the rarest of the Timuri rugs of East Persia and West Afghanistan. Few antique examples are known, but occasionally a late 19th century or early 20th century piece will appear on the market. All have a similar field design of vertical rectangular medallions, but colours such as the light blue of the central medallion, and the light blue and green of motifs in the main border, as well as in the outlines of design elements in the field of this carpet, are much better in the old pieces. Note the striking use of white wool outlining the top and bottom central medallions of the field and the fine reciprocal trefoil guard stripes enclosing the field and major border. Perhaps these were the ceremonial and presentation pieces made especially for tribal leaders or others of like importance.

TECHNICAL ANALYSIS
Warp: Z2S, ivory wool, alternate warps slightly depressed.
Weft: 2Z, two shoots dark brown and black wool.
Pile: 2Z, wool, Persian knot open to left, 96 knots per sq. in.
Selvage: Not original.
Ends: Reduced; remaining striped plain-weave kilim with a half inch band in weft-
  float technique.
Colours: Light red, light blue, dark blue, gold, dark green, apricot, violet-brown, dark brown
  (corroded), and white (bleached wool).
Literature: See *Rare Oriental Carpets VII* by Eberhart Herrmann, Munich 1985, plate 70.

PLATE 55

TIMURI RUG,
Northwest Afghanistan, Herat province, Gulran district,
circa 1870.
3′7″ × 5′11″.

AS WITH THE PREVIOUS EXAMPLE, here we find the rich colours
representing the best naturally dyed wool which has become so very rare.
This rug, however, has several features which set it apart from others in
this group, including its small size for the type; the dissimilar design of the
three central medallions of the field; the head to head reproduction of the
weaver and her shadow in the upper right corner of the field; the attractive
light and medium blue abrash in the mainly dark blue of the field; the
dominant, but very simplified, form of the 'S' motifs in the major border;
and the unusual irregularity of the borders in the right central section. This
last feature leads one to wonder how this could have occurred in an
otherwise perfectly woven example. Perhaps the weaver had an assistant
(a young child?) working alongside her at this point.

TECHNICAL ANALYSIS
Warp: Z2S, ivory wool, level back.
Weft: 2Z, two, sometimes three, shoots dark brown wool.
Pile: 2Z, wool, Persian knot open to left, 80 knots per sq. in.
Selvage: Two cables, (Z2S)12Z, wrapped in dark brown wool.
Ends: Six inch striped plain-weave kilim decorated with a one inch central weft-float band
    with chain-stitch guard stripes.
Colours: Light coral-red, medium red, light blue, medium blue, dark blue, blue-green, light
    brown (corroded), dark brown, gold, black (corroded), and ivory.

PLATE 56

TIMURI SADDLE BAG,
Northwest Afghanistan, Herat province, Gulran district,
late 19th century.
2'6" × 4'9".

THE LUSTROUS PILED FACES of this saddle bag have a deep blue
field filled with tree-like ornaments in pomegranate-red, light blue and
blue-green, with a few details in apricot-brown and ivory. The tree designs
are similar to those used by the Dokhtar-e-Ghazi of northwestern
Afghanistan in the field of their prayer rugs, but the structure, colouring
and silky wool of traditional Timuri tribal weavings predominate. The
directional leafy vine (arrowheads) of the border also suggest Timuri
workmanship from western Afghanistan. Note the variation between the
filler motifs of each face and the change in border design on one face.

TECHNICAL ANALYSIS
Warp: Z2S, ivory wool, level back.
Weft: 2Z, two shoots light brown wool.
Pile: 2Z, wool, Persian knot open to left, 48 knots per sq. in.
Selvage: Sides closed with a raised fish-bone stitch in dark brown goat hair.
Ends: One and a half inch plain-weave kilim band with closure slits bounded by a thin band of
    ivory weft-float and lines of weft twining. Braided dark brown goat hair closure loops are
    twined into the plain-weave back. Warp ends turned under and sewn down.
Colours: Pomegranate-red, apricot-brown, light brown, dark brown, light blue, dark blue,
    blue-green, and ivory.
Published: HALI, Vol. 3, no. 1, London 1980, p. 35, fig. 6.

PLATE 57

AIMAQ RUG, DOKHTAR-E-GHAZI,
Northwest Afghanistan, Herat province, Gulran area,
mid 19th century.
3'0" × 5'8".

IDENTIFIABLE WEAVINGS of the Dokhtar-e-Ghazi, except prayer
rugs and bags, are rare. This piece is thought to be either Dokhtar-e-Ghazi
or Timuri. Since these groups appear to be related and no known Timuri
rug has this plant design, the rug is attributed to the former group. The
basic field design of three vertical panels, one black and the other two
woven in a clear light red is also unusual. The black, which is corroded, has
been repaired in several places with dark brown wool. The principal
design in the major border consists of a brown-violet chain connecting
quartered diamond forms. Small blue and red geometric motifs fill the
voids. The ivory and red reciprocal trefoil minor borders highlight the
frame of the field, while the red and blue inner border is rendered in the
'ocean wave' pattern. It is interesting to note that the weaver started to
weave the field in alternating blocks of wave and plant forms but changed
after one row to the simple plant form which covers the field. The piece is
woven in fine, soft, lustrous wool.

TECHNICAL ANALYSIS
Warp: Z2S, ivory wool, level back.
Weft: 2Z, two shoots dark brown wool.
Pile: 2Z, wool, Persian knot open to left, 104 knots per sq. in.
Selvage: Not original; sides overcast in dark brown wool.
Ends: Two and a half inch band in soumak technique.
Colours: Clear light red, coral-red, light blue, dark blue, brown-violet, gold, dark brown,
   black (corroded), and ivory.

PLATE 58

TIMURI SADDLE BAG, DOKHTAR-E-GHAZI,
Northwest Afghanistan, Herat province, Gulran area,
late 19th century.
2'6" × 5'5".

THE PILE FACES of this bag are closely knotted with an uncommonly silky wool. The dominant feature of the design decorating the medium blue field is a light cherry-red octagon with a central smaller ivory octagon enclosing an eight-pointed star. According to Dr Jon Thompson, in his commentary on a similar saddle bag face in *Rugs of the Wandering Baluchi* (plate 18), the medium blue motifs projecting towards the central star from the short diagonal sides of the large octagon may represent stylized animals or birds facing a tree. These design elements, which appear on certain Turkish rugs of the 14th and 15th centuries, may be a relic of ancient contacts with Turkic steppe nomads. The field surrounding this large octagon is filled with the familiar tree-like forms found in Dokhtar-e-Ghazi prayer rugs. The major ivory border is filled with repeating floral stems bearing pairs of opposed leaves and diamond flowers in full bloom. A small, carefully executed, reciprocal trefoil inner border frames the field. A one inch band of red weft-float has been added to the bottom of each piled face. Multicoloured wool and goat hair tassels are added to this band and the sides of the piece. The precise designs, beautiful, soft, silky wool, and excellent dyes make this an outstanding example of tribal art.

TECHNICAL ANALYSIS
Warp: Z2S, ivory wool, level back.
Weft: 2Z, two shoots light brown wool.
Pile: 2Z, wool, Persian knot open to left, 108 knots per sq. in.
Selvage: Sides closed with a raised fish-bone stitch in dark brown goat hair.
Ends: One and a half inch plain-weave kilim band with closure slits. Each closure section is decorated with a stylized weft-float flower and is bounded by thin bands of ivory and red weft-float and lines of chain-stitch. Braided red and brown wool closure loops plus three dark brown goat hair loops are twined into the plain-weave back. The warp ends are turned under and sewn down. The ends, both front and back, of the striped bridge section are reinforced with wide bands of braided dark brown goat hair.
Colours: Light cherry-red, blue-green, medium blue, dark blue, violet-brown, and ivory (bleached).

PLATE 59

TIMURI CARPET,
Northwest Afghanistan, Herat province, Kushk district,
late 19th century.
5'7" × 8'2".

ANOTHER OUTSTANDING EXAMPLE of Timuri weaving with rich,
dark colours and fine, lustrous wool. This carpet originally had elaborate
weft-float ends and heavy six-cable selvages of dark brown goat hair. The
selvages were badly damaged and were removed when the piece was
repaired, as were the ragged portions of the kilim ends. The carpet has a
number of attractive features. Overall it has a fascinating, lustrous, bluish-
red appearance when light strikes the fine, soft wool. This feature, plus its
typical design elements, prompted many people in the late 19th and early
20th centuries to refer to such rugs as 'Blue Bokharas'. Additional interest
is provided by ivory highlights throughout and a few touches of mauve in
the centre of some flower heads. The black dye was caustic and corroded
the wool, making it brittle and worn and giving the piece a carved
appearance. Note the four pairs of small animals (probably goats) in the
main border.

TECHNICAL ANALYSIS
Warp: Z2S, ivory wool, level back.
Weft: 2Z, two shoots dark brown wool.
Pile: 2Z, wool, Persian knot open to left, 70 knots per sq. in.
Selvages: Missing.
Ends: Reduced; remaining one inch band of plain-weave decorated with weft-float guarded
on each side by two rows of weft twining.
Colours: Light red, dark wine-red, medium blue, medium blue-green, black (corroded),
mauve, and ivory.
Literature: See *Tapis de l'Asie Centrale* by General A.A. Bogolrouboff, St. Petersburg 1908,
plate XXXI.

PLATE 60

TIMURI CARPET,
Northwest Afghanistan, Herat province, Kushk district,
mid 19th century.
6'7" × 7'11".

THE MEDIUM BLUE FIELD with three vertical rows of stylized, stepped floral major güls separated by two rows of hooked minor güls, is arranged by colours to produce a diagonal effect. Three peacocks – two ivory and one red – appear in the violet-brown major border. Striking, clear, light red and snowy white colours highlight the piece. This carpet, closely knotted in fine, silky wool dyed in excellent colours is an outstanding example of the finest Timuri work.

TECHNICAL ANALYSIS
Warp: Z2S, ivory wool, alternate warps slightly depressed.
Weft: 2Z, one or two shoots dark brown wool.
Pile: 2Z, wool, Persian knot open to left, 80 knots per sq. in.
Selvage: Not original.
Ends: Missing.
Colours: Clear light red, brown-red, violet-brown, dark brown (corroded), black (corroded), medium blue, apricot, and ivory (bleached wool).

PLATE 61

AIMAQ, KAUDANI TIMURI SADDLE BAG (HALF),
Northwest Afghanistan, Herat province, Kushk district,
late 19th century.
2′3″ × 2′3″.

THE PEACOCK MOTIF appears in Baluchi and Baluchi type weaving over a wide area of the Khorasan and Herat provinces of eastern Persia and western Afghanistan. In this instance the dark blue ground of the field contains nine peacocks arranged in horizontal and vertical rows of three each. The central bird is in ivory, the end birds in the upper and lower horizontal rows are in light red while the middle birds in the outer rows are in a dark violet-brown which renders them almost invisible against the dark blue ground. The light red major border is filled with a chain of dark blue and violet-brown eight-pointed stars. The minor border contains reciprocal stepped half diamond forms in the colours of the field. This border is guarded by thin beaded lines in gold. The sides of the bag are closed by a fish-bone stitch in dark brown goat hair.

TECHNICAL ANALYSIS
Warp: Z2S, ivory wool, level back.
Weft: 2Z, two shoots dark brown wool.
Pile: 2Z, wool, Persian knot open to left, 70 knots per sq. in.
Selvage: Two cables of two warps each. Sides originally closed with dark brown goat hair in the raised fish-bone stitch (now mostly missing).
Ends: Three inch plain-weave kilim with slits for closure and a quarter inch band of ivory weft-float.
Colours: Light red, medium blue, dark blue, violet-brown, gold, and ivory.

PLATE 62

AIMAQ RUG, MAUDUDI-JAMSHIDI,
Northwest Afghanistan, Herat province, Kushk district,
late 19th century.
2'8" × 11'0".

THIS LONG SIDE RUG was probably made for a person of importance, considering the dyes used and the care exercised in its construction. The light reddish-brown field is decorated with a chain of six curvilinear 'latch-hook' diamond medallions with the beginning of a seventh at the top – all with a central cruciform motif in a corroded olive-brown wool which presents a carved effect due to the decrease in pile height. The narrow ivory main border is filled with a chain of perfectly drawn eight-pointed star-in-octagons and is separated from the outer coral-red and inner medium blue 'ocean-wave' secondary borders by barber pole stripes. This main border, plus the curvilinear design in the field and the Turkish knot in which the piece is woven indicate that the weaver was a member of a Turkic group. It is well known that some clans of the Chahar Aimaq include people of Turkic as well as Persian, Mongol and Arab extraction.

TECHNICAL ANALYSIS
Warp: Z2S, ivory wool, alternate warps moderately depressed.
Weft: 2Z, two shoots brown wool.
Pile: 2Z, wool, Turkish knot points to right, 80 knots per sq. in.
Selvage: Four cables, (Z2S)3Z, bound into a two-cord selvage with dark brown goat hair.
Ends: Reduced; plain striped kilim.
Colours: Coral-red, light reddish-brown, medium blue, dark blue, violet-brown, medium green, olive-brown (corroded), dark brown, and ivory.
Literature: See 'The So-Called Herat Baluch Rugs and Their Weavers' by Alfred Janata, in *Oriental Carpet & Textile Studies*, Vol. I, edited by Robert Pinner and Walter B. Denny, London 1985, fig. 1.

PLATE 63

AIMAQ SADDLE BAG, JAMSHIDI,
Northwest Afghanistan, Herat province, Kushk area,
circa 1880.
2′4″ × 4′8″.

THE FIELD DESIGN in the lustrous pile faces of this saddle bag is unique in that it is usually found decorating rugs. The principal feature is the single, large, medium blue, diamond shaped, curvilinear 'latch-hook' medallion with an inner band of latch-hooks outlined in an electric light blue. This medallion encloses three concentric serrated diamond forms in light blue and cherry-red on a violet-brown ground. The dominant colour is the electric light blue outlining the latch-hooks and the floral tendrils sprouting from the diamond points of the medallion. The medium blue field is framed by a reciprocal split-tendril major border in cherry-red and violet-brown outlined in blue. The fine coral-red floral vine inner border serves to provide a further highlight to the piece.

TECHNICAL ANALYSIS
Warp: Z2S, ivory wool, level back.
Weft: 2Z, two, sometimes three, shoots light brown wool.
Pile: 2Z, wool, Persian knot open to left, 70 knots per sq. in.
Selvage: Two cables, (Z2S)2Z, wrapped in dark brown wool. Sides closed with a raised fish-bone stitch in dark brown goat hair (missing in places).
Ends: Upper two inch band of plain-weave with slits for closure bounded by a thin band of weft-float and lines of weft twining. Braided dark brown goat hair closure loops are twined into the plain-weave back.
Colours: Cherry-red, coral-red, light blue, medium blue, light brown, and violet-brown (corroded).

PLATE 64

AIMAQ PRAYER RUG, JAMSHIDI,
Northwest Afghanistan, Herat province, Kushk district,
early 20th century.
3'1" × 5'3".

THE LIGHT BROWN FIELD AND SPANDRELS, like those of the preceding example, contain curvilinear 'latch-hook' medallions. It is also decorated with a broad ivory main border, but in this case filled with alternating Turkoman *Ashik* güls and triple ended bars which indicate a Turkic background for the weaver. The narrow inner border is filled with a continuous row of black, red, and green birds' head motifs and the interior of the prayer arch contains two square box-flower designs of four blossoms each. An unusual feature for rugs of this type are the broad, plain-woven kilim ends or skirts decorated in the colours of the field.

TECHNICAL ANALYSIS
Warp: Z2S, ivory wool, alternate warps moderately depressed.
Weft: 2Z, two shoots brown wool.
Pile: 2Z, wool, Turkish knot points to left, woven top end first, 80 knots per sq. in.
Selvage: Four cables, Z4S, ivory wool wrapped in dark brown goat hair.
Ends: Top – six inch; bottom – five inch, plain, interlocked kilim in deep toothed design with a
  band of brown weft-float 'ocean wave' forms.
Colours: Light coral-red, brown-red, brown-violet, light blue, dark blue, blue-green, light
  brown, dark brown, and ivory.

PLATE 65

AIMAQ RUG,
West Afghanistan, Herat province, south Gurian area,
late 19th century.
2'10" × 5'7".

SEVERAL FEATURES OF THIS RUG make it rare for a Baluchi type weaving. For example, the light coral-red secondary borders in the rare chain diamond form; and the stylized floral plant motif in the field together with the overall light colours which are more indicative of Sistan weavings. Note how the plant forms stand out from the field in a sculpted manner as a result of pile wear caused by the corrosive, caustic effect of the olive-brown dye. Also unusual is the diagonal pattern of the plants in the field from upper right to lower left – the reverse of the usual form found in Baluchi weaving. Finally, note that the light brown coloured plants of the fourth diagonal row were originally purple-violet but have now faded leaving the blue-green outlines. After thoroughly reviewing weavings from the area and the analysis listed below, the rug was assigned to the southwest border area of Herat province. It is thought that the weaver may be related to the Bahluris of the Qainat area of south Khorasan in Persia.

TECHNICAL ANALYSIS
Warp: Z2S, ivory wool, level back.
Weft: 2Z, two shoots mixed wool and goat hair.
Pile: 2Z, wool, Turkish knot points to right, 70 knots per sq. in.
Selvage: Two cables, Z4, wrapped in dark brown goat hair.
Ends: Four inch striped plain-weave kilim.
Colours: Light coral-red, medium blue, dark blue, blue-green, purple-violet (tip faded to light brown), light olive-brown (corroded), dark brown, and ivory.
Literature: See *Rare Oriental Carpets VI* by Eberhart Herrmann, Munich 1984, plate 74.

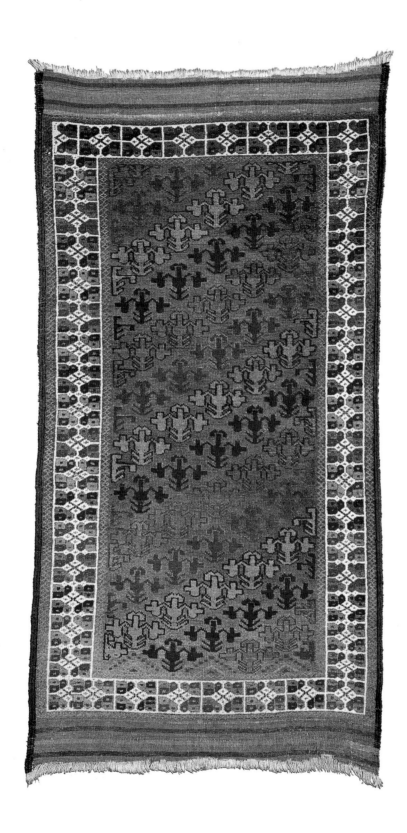

BIBLIOGRAPHY

Azadi, S., *Carpets in the Baluch Tradition*, Munich 1986.

Bausback, P., *Alte Knüpfarbeiten der Belutschen*, Mannheim 1980.

Bennett, I., 'On Collecting Baluch Rugs – Mainly for Pleasure', in *Hali*, Vol. 3, no. 1, 1980.

Black, D. and Loveless, C., *Rugs of the Wandering Baluchi*, London 1976.

Bogoliouboff, A.A., *Tapis de l'Asie Centrale*, St Petersburg 1908. (English trans., *Carpets of Central Asia*, annotated by J.M.A. Thompson, Wheathold Green 1973).

Boucher, J.W., 'Baluchi Weaving of the 19th Century', in *Hali*, Vol. 1, no. 3, 1978.

Cammann, S.V.R., 'Symbolic Meaning in Oriental Rug Patterns, Part I, in *The Textile Museum Journal*, Vol. III, no. 3, Washington D.C. 1972.

Craycraft, M., *Belouch Prayer Rugs*, Point Reyes Station 1982.

Dimand, M.S., *Ballard Collection of Oriental Rugs in the City Art Museum of St. Louis*, 1935.

Dupree, L., *Afghanistan*, Princeton 1973.

Edwards, A.C., *The Persian Carpet*, London 1953.

Frye, R.W., 'Remarks on Baluchi History', in *Central Asiatic Journal*, London 1961.

Herrmann, E., *Rare Oriental Carpets*, Vol. VI, Munich 1984.

Herrmann, E., *Rare Oriental Carpets*, Vol. VII, Munich 1985.

Hopf, A., *Oriental Carpets and Rugs*, London 1962.

Janata, A., 'Textilien der Aimak aus Zentralasien', in *Hali*, Vol. 2, no. 3, 1979.

Janata, A., 'The So-Called Herat Baluch Rugs and Their Weavers', in *Oriental Carpet & Textile Studies*, Vol. I, Ed. R. Pinner & W.B. Denny, London 1985.

Jones, H.M. and Boucher, J.W., *Baluchi Rugs*, The International Hajji Baba Society, Inc., Washington D.C. 1974.

Lefevre, J., *The Persian Carpet*, London 1977.

Landreau, A.N., Ed., *Yoruk – The Nomadic Weaving Tradition of the Middle East*, Pittsburg 1978.

Longworth Dames, M., 'Balocistan', in: *Encyclopaedia of Islam*, Vol. I, A-D, 1913.

O'Bannon, G.W., 'Baluchi Rugs', in Landreau, *op. cit.*

Pottinger, H., *Travels in Belouchistan and Sinde*, London 1816.

Tate, G.P., *The Frontiers of Baluchistan*, London 1909.

Thacher, A.B., *Turkoman Rugs*, New York 1940.

Wegner, D.H.G., 'Some Notes on the Rugs of Baluchi Nomads and Related Weavers', in *Hali*, Vol. 1, no. 3, 1978.

Wegner, D.H.G., 'Der Knüpfteppich bei den Belutschen und ihren Nachbarn', in *Tribus*, No. 29, Stuttgart 1980. (English trans., 'Pile Rugs of the Balouch and Their Neighbors', in *Oriental Rug Review*, Vol. V, nos. 4-8, Meredith, N.H. 1985).